To: Am

CONSCIOUS LEADERSHIP
7 Principles That WILL Change Your Business and Change Your Life

Michael Bianco-Splann

Life is not for the faint of heart. The journey we take is short and filled with endless opportunities and challenges. But its in the challenge that we find ourselves, evolving, growing and better able to choose light over darkness.

I wish you light & love— And I stand with you on the journey. With love & friendship)

Michael

Conscious Leadership: 7 Principles That WILL Change Your Business and Change Your Life

Visit the author website:
www.illuminateambitions.com

Cover design: River Coyote Design
www.rivercoyotedesign.com

Author website: River Coyote Design
www.rivercoyotedesign.com

ISBN: 978-0-9962296-0-9 (paperback)
ISBN: 978-0-9962296-1-6 (ebook)

Printed by: IngramSpark
www.ingramspark.com

Contents

Conscious Leadership
7 Principles that WILL Change your Business and Change Your Life

Foreword One

You are holding an important book. A life-changing book. If you are already a leader, this book will change the way you think about yourself, your vision, your purpose, and your passion. If you don't define yourself as a leader, reading this book just may surprise you as you glimpse yourself in aspects of leadership you've never acknowledged, described in its pages and defined in new and evolutionary ways. And if you're not yet a leader but wish to become one, then this book is written especially for you. Let it be your handbook, your guide to creating in yourself the transformational leader so needed in today's world. If you are stepping into leadership now, amidst the chaos and confusion, and have chosen to read this book, kudos to you. You are right on time.

Michael Bianco-Splann is a remarkable person, and has written a remarkable book. In it you will find not one untruth or misdirection, not one word written without conscious intention and in full integrity, and not one example or anecdote not personally experienced by Michael himself. He writes from what he knows, which is immense, and he practices what he teaches. Michael's leadership is conscious and inspired and passionate and aware, evolved and revolutionary. And, in these pages, completely lucid and accessible. He is an excellent communicator and his principles are profound in their simplicity. Be kind. Know yourself. Care about others. Question the Powers That Be. Lead in a way that lets you sleep at night. Cultivate Peace. Michael's commitment to these values in his work and in his life puts him side by side with the greatest leaders of our time, leaders he refers to in the book, but is much too humble to compare himself with. Trust me, he's in their league.

You don't need an MBA or a Ph.D. to appreciate this book and put it to work in your life. As Michael and I have discussed many times, everyone leads. Be it in their family, their community, their workplace, their planet, at some point everyone must lead. These 7 principles are usable by everyone and will benefit everyone who spends time getting to know them and put them into practice.

I believe that in the deep uncertainty that is the 21st Century, we are all called to be leaders of the highest kind, the kind Michael's principles foster. Conscious, pro-active, and aware. And most importantly, leaders who are passionate and alive once more, shining the light of conscious leadership as a beacon to the leaders of tomorrow.

Enjoy this book. It's a treasure. And give it to the people you love to let them know who you are at your deepest core, what you value, and the potential you recognize in them to also be powerful, effective, conscious leaders.

You never know where the next great world-changer might come from. As Michael passionately espouses, look in the mirror. It might just be you.

Janice Stefanacci Seward, PSY.D.
Doctor of Psychology
Clinical Professor of Psychological Medicine
Founder and President of *Fruition Dynamic Change Services*
and *Embody Healing Arts*

Great Barrington MA, April 2015

Conscious Leadership
7 Principles that WILL Change your Business and Change Your Life

Foreword Two

Conscious Leadership is a power book that invites the reader to become self-aware and reminds us that human connections are the energy source for sustainable success. I have known Michael Bianco-Splann for many years and seen his tenacious, yet kind manner positively drive high volume sales production in global financial institutions. Michael's success is consistently related to people connections, which inspire exceptional performance. It's no surprise that he ultimately decided to capture his experiences in a book for others to learn, grow, and discover leadership principles.

The book is deeply authentic and reminds us that our contribution to others is greater than titles or company scorecards. Sustained success is the experience of teaching others to have "genuine connections" that make us better human beings. While reading the book, I found myself pausing on several occasions to ask critical questions and reflect on my own professional journey.

I was reminded of a time many years ago when I first saw Michael standing in front of a group of new Retail Bankers, facilitating a training class on customer interaction mastery. I remember the faces of the participants, many of which looked as though they had recently discovered self-confidence. I stood in awe as Michael leveraged relatable experiences and remembered nuances about each participant that engaged them to learn an important skill centered on building relationships with others.

Afterwards, we had lunch and it was obvious he lived many of the principles his book describes, by sharing proud moments of connecting with class participants. In that moment, I knew Michael would certainly excel as a human being and professional, because he demonstrated connectivity starts with active listening.

Since that time, Michael has consistently demonstrated that leadership requires the commitment to inspire others by foremost becoming self-comfortable.

"Conscious Leadership" reminds us to tap into the skills we all possess. It's no doubt that each reader will self-discover important moments about their life journey and become better prepared for deeply authentic relationships. This book is a must read for now and many years to come.

Michael T. Pugh
President and Chief Executive Officer
Carver Federal Savings Bank

Conscious Leadership
7 Principles that WILL Change your Business and Change Your Life

Acknowledgments

Many of us have callings or internal nudges that impel us to dance differently, urging us to stop and listen or take action. And it is easy to scoff and throw away these intuitive pings as false flags or our imaginations gone wild. Yet, if we were truthful to ourselves, we would embrace these messages or ripples in our state of being, not merely as a rock thrown into a serene pool of water, but more importantly from the vantage point of capturing the energy that flows from the ripples across the smooth surface of our individual and collective complacency.

Conscious Leadership demands our attention. In an ever-shrinking world brought even closer as a result of the incredible power of the worldwide web, one thing remains a constant—change. Over the past two decades, I have been fortunate to experience wonderful learning and growth in my own leadership development. This book is the culmination of my experiences, good, bad and indifferent. The transition from manager to effective conscious leader has been replete with great successes and challenging failures. But out of my journey has emerged a strong and confident belief that in order to be the change-maker, the peace-builder, the advocate and the type of leader, husband, father, friend and human being needed in our present world of dysfunction, violence, inequality, greed and human toil, I must take action.

I am the composite of the managers and leaders who span the gamut of ability. From extremely talented to massively incompetent, I have assimilated skills, attributes and styles of outstanding leaders while choosing to discard those with limited and self-aggrandizing styles of management. Knowing what not to do as a leader is equally as important as knowing what and how to lead. Unfortunately, so many leaders are caught in the trap of fear and organizational malaise, for to raise an issue or question the established norms, is risky business. Fear of job loss, retaliation and being classified as a troublemaker or naysayer all leave today's leader in a vexing and uncomfortable position.

The Seven Principles outlined in this book highlight
essential ways of being. They are wakeup calls to leaders
from across all lines of business, from fortune 100
companies to small boutique enterprise. Any forum in
which you, as leader, are called to guide and coalesce
human activity for an express purpose or result demands
a different dance. And the dance steps called for are
those that speak to the exponential evolution occurring
at every level of our collective existence. The next great
opportunity for us as a human family is in raising our
consciousness, for it is conscious evolution that has
morphed from the survival-of-the-fittest.

The win-lose indelible construct we live by in our current
condition only takes us so far. And in the pursuit of this
mainstream belief system, we have created a country and
world supporting a view of separate and apart. In this
view of the world and our place in it, we see a widening
of income inequality and the ravages of poverty. We see
educational systems woefully inept, out-of-touch and
ineffective in providing the necessary learning to equip
our students to carry the gauntlet into a new world. We
see a polarized political system with complete stalemate
in our government's ability to support its citizens. We see
global violence that engulfs the entire Middle East. We
are witnessing the destruction of mother Earth,

evidenced by the melting of our polar icecaps, the extinction of insect and animal species, extreme prolonged droughts and severe changing weather patterns, largely the result of carbon-based fuel consumption and the collective psychosis attached to arguing the certainty of our demise. We are beyond the tipping point. Further accelerating our tenuous position are the corporate structures that put profits ahead of health and wellbeing. The time for all of us to answer the individual and collective stirrings is now.

It is with supreme grace and gratitude that this book is written. Those leaders who have impacted me viscerally with their messages of peace, equality, justice, compassion and love are to be acknowledged. Such individuals as Dr. Martin Luther King, Jr., John F. Kennedy, Nelson Mandela, Gandhi, Rosa Parks, Eleanor Roosevelt and Susan B. Anthony are just a few of the leaders who have impacted me so profoundly. In my own professional capacity, leaders such as Robert Curley, NY Chairman of the Board with Berkshire Bank, continues to demonstrate a passionate caring for everyone he touches, bringing compassion, vision and a wonderful sense of humor to the work environment. My collaboration with Tony Penn, CEO of United Way of Tucson and Southern Arizona, is an example of extraordinary leadership within the non-profit sector in bridging great differences to harness amazing results. I have been so fortunate to work with these types of conscious leaders.

But leadership comes in many forms, not just in the corporate world. Leadership is ubiquitous, encompassing parents, grandparents, educators, ministry, community and social justice advocates, the arts, medical professionals, and anyone who connects with others. These are the many faces of leaders, from small to very large; they all have one thing in common, the human connection.

I have experienced great fortune in my professional and personal associations established over the past many years. One exceptional guide, teacher, coach and friend who has been a strong advocate for realizing my own potential is Dr. Janice Stefanacci-Seward. As my Life Coach and advocate, Dr. Jan has been instrumental in supporting my own journey from fear to full self-expression and potential. Her unwavering guidance has remained a driving force to my moving from corporate to pursue my calling.

Several years ago while working through a very challenging time period, it was Dr. Jan who prompted my pursuit of a master's degree in transpersonal leadership at Atlantic University. Taking one class per semester while continuing to work within the financial services industry, I have been able to amass great learning and perspectives that infuse the content of my writing and the passions of my heart. Expanding the boundaries of learning to embrace alternative ways of knowing, aligning the heart with the mind, realizing that in order to bridge differences one must set aside rigid belief systems to understand our shared humanity are but a few of the insights of learning afforded me from Atlantic University. To Director, James Van Auken and the talented faculty, I express my gratitude and thanks.

Another critically important nugget of personal experience impacting my professional leadership development over time has been the blessing of being a parent. Yes, it is with great appreciation that I acknowledge the indispensible learning that comes from parenting children. As the father of a blended family of three boys, coming to the realization that the world does not revolve around me but rather them, has opened the door to a level of love, patience and presence I otherwise would never know. I especially appreciate my son,

Matthew, for his unwavering encouragement, support and belief in me. Clearly, his undying and relentless optimism has been a wonderful support in realizing my own potential.

Finally and most importantly, I give honor and appreciation to my wife, partner and best friend, Janeen, whose soulful dedication and loving support continues to be the wind beneath my wings. I am the lock and she is the key. Without her strong expertise and unselfish generosity, there would be no book nor would there be the incredible enthusiasm for the collaborative work ahead. Truly, she is a gift of the divine.

After working in the professional world for over three decades, taking the step across the threshold into my work with clients as their Life Coach, my collaboration with leaders and organizations to infuse consciousness into their lifeblood, and in evangelizing a new way to lead others, I extend an invitation to all readers for a bright and conscious future.

What you do is important, but *how* you do *what* you do will determine not only your future, but also profoundly impact those you lead and serve.

Welcome to **consciousness.**

Conscious Leadership
7 Principles That WILL Change Your Business and Change Your Life

INTRODUCTION

We all have the extraordinary coded within us, waiting to be released

~Jean Houston

We sauntered into the conference room like lieutenants gathering for a mission briefing. Once again, we were gathering for our executive meeting to discuss our progress toward financial goals, share best practices, tacitly entertain challenges, and listen to the newest iteration of company expectations. What we did know was that no matter how well we were producing against corporate goals, the overarching message was *more*: more productivity, more output, more with less resources, more expectations placed on all of us as leaders of our business. *More* is the perpetual corporate mantra month after month, quarter after quarter, year after year.

This commonplace ritual of aligning corporate strategy to create an environment of high performance told the story of our failing to do enough yet again. Something is missing from a leadership model that leaves leaders feeling unrecognized, unfulfilled, and chronically lacking--even those who perform well. The unfortunate reality is that we are never satisfied with ourselves, constantly feeling the gnawing angst of falling behind, missing a mark, forgetting one of hundreds of deliverables, and ultimately enduring rather than living true to our passion and purpose. Many of us wonder: Where have my dreams and aspirations gone? Am I fulfilled? Do I have a level of happiness and satisfaction that aligns to my true and authentic self?

As I participate in the corporate dance, it becomes clear to me that we are but a group of talking heads, nodding with acquiescence at senior leaders, forever toeing the line. Such leaders dole out what they believe is strategic and motivational communication to encourage us to produce more while living up to a corporate mission and satisfying Wall Street and shareholders. What becomes clear through the fog of untruth is our casual acceptance of this way of life as normal and ultimately out of our control.

What is truth? What is your truth? So often I ponder this important question while viewing corporate media extolling stories of doom and gloom, observing with distain the political gridlock in Washington and the tempest of violent brutality raging in the Middle East. Truth becomes an elusive shadow that demands our attention and action. But to wake up requires changing the story to gain control.

The truth is that we are living unconsciously, well below our potential as leaders and human beings, just skimming the surface of what is achievable. I have often witnessed good people deadened by their leadership output falling on deaf ears, with their own energy sapped by endless hours of executing the corporate playbook only to find unmotivated employees doing just enough to get by. The personal toll of living an unfulfilled professional life in which success is measured by the degree to which one drinks the corporate elixir can be immeasurably destructive.

Early on in my banking career, while working as the Director of Training for a financial services organization that was transforming from a savings and thrift to a sales-driven retail bank, I caught myself during a leadership training program referring to the company as *them*. It dawned on me at that moment that *them* was in fact *me*. I was the architect, the decision- maker. What I produced and how I led those I touched was, in truth, the company speaking. And as long as I aligned my goals with those of the company, there were limits to my ability to foster meaningful change and impact.

I woke up and realized that this thing called life is not a dress rehearsal. It's the *real thing*. After decades of working within this corporate maze, I knew I needed to make some important choices. One choice was to acknowledge the falseness of the corporate world and consciously move toward a professional aspiration of supporting others in realizing their own self-expression. Another choice was to look inside my own psycho-spiritual world, as well as inside the system to which I professionally contribute, to find pearls of opportunity for conscious leadership.

Conscious leadership is waking up, moving away from autopilot management to embrace an awareness of oneself in relationship to those being served, both associates as well as customers.

My journey has evolved significantly over the past five years. Moving across the country from New York to

Tucson, then to Atlanta and finally to Los Angeles while changing companies three times has provided me a rich, yet challenging level of experience culminating in an awakening to the awareness of my own passionate callings and ultimately a decision to leave the banking industry.

Working within the financial services industry for sixteen years afforded me great learning, the most impactful being the realization that I am more than just a cog in the wheel of leading others, more than an unconscious professional, more than what I am told I am by the company that employs me. I am a human being in control of my own destiny. The choices I exercise are mine to make. The question becomes, what choices am I making in my roles as leader, husband, father, friend and brother to all others? And in the exercise of my choices, am I conscious of living where life is actually occurring—right here, right now?

This book addresses two sides of the same coin. On one side is my working within the system to shed light on the rote practice of leading others according to the corporate model and playbook--in short, pushing them to do more and feel chronically insufficient. The seven principles offered in this book have emerged directly from my experience as a corporate leader. Consciously employing these principles has provided me with unique and powerful tools that I believe others will find rich and rewarding in their own leadership practices.

On the other side, being true to my own inner calling as an authentic source of supporting others to realize their full potential, has led me to choose to leave the corporate world and form my own company, Illuminate Ambitions.

As a certified transformational life coach, motivational speaker and performance consultant, my aim is to provide individuals and organizations with a full range of coaching, training and support in bringing the light of consciousness to others. Shining the light of conscious leadership is not only the next great step in leading others but is a call to those of us who care about our associates, our loved ones, our communities and the greater human family.

While much of the material speaks to the corporate leader, its application is immediately relevant to anyone seeking to live fully self-expressed, powerful and with the joy of love, compassion and greater understanding. Be the light you are!

The message is equally aligned to organizations seeking to improve bottom line revenue, corporate earnings, employee engagement and a differentiated customer satisfaction. My strong experience in performance consulting and training provides organizations with a dynamic resource for significantly enhancing organizational performance.

The 7 Principles of Conscious Leadership elucidate patterns of living that encompass the whole person, not just as a leader but in all facets of our lives. We are more than what our professional title or our personal possessions say we are. In my current professional capacity, I have embraced these principles to realize much greater harmony with my authentic self--the *real* me. The result has been a significant increase in my overall emotional balance, as I align my actions and behaviors to genuinely serve those I lead.

It is within everyone's ability to switch on the energy that allows us to live consciously and step into leadership as a limitless enterprise. The first step is to know thyself.

Conscious Leadership Principle #1:
BE THE REAL YOU

By the time you are Real, most of your hair has been loved off, and your eyes drop out and you get loose in the joints and very shabby. But these things don't matter at all, because once you are Real you can't be ugly, except to people who don't understand....Once you are Real you can't become unreal again. It lasts for always.

~Margery Williams, *The Velveteen Rabbit*

In a variety of interactions, from one-on-one conversations to large-group presentations, I pose the question: "Why do bankers (fill in the blank with whatever corporate title fits) come to work, hang their personalities on a hook, and become 'bankers?'" The smiles and laughs that follow suggest an instant recognition of the truth.

What does it mean to be a banker, lawyer, doctor, educator, not-for-profit leader, or any other professional? For many people, it is a debilitating experience of separating our genuinely loving, warm, compassionate selves from the hard, ruthless, determined-to-win persona that is demanded in our workplace.

Yet, do we truly realize what is left behind when we separate our true selves from our professional roles? We are abandoning what is uniquely wonderful about us, those parts of ourselves that others desperately want from us: honesty, authenticity, and genuine human connection.

SAME TITLE, SAME PLAYBOOK, DIFFERENT RESULTS

Have you ever wondered why ten different people can have the exact same script or sequence of events and have ten completely different outcomes? Why do some find success while others fail? The answer lies not in what you are saying, doing, or showing, but rather in *how* you are connecting with other human beings.

Take Melissa, a newer Personal Banker, who delivers consistently outstanding sales results in the flow of her daily performance. She is one of thirty-five Personal

Bankers executing against the exact corporate playbook, yet her results are double those of her peers--same products, same services and same training, with very different outcomes. Melissa's success is the composite of her internal motivation as well as her ability to connect with others from a compassionate and empathetic heart.

Then there is Wesley, a young leader brought into a struggling banking center where the previous leader had created a harshly critical and polarized workforce, largely the result of his narcissistic insistence that "it's my way or the highway." Wesley immediately installed strong accountability and imparted a genuine sense of caring, empathy and compassion to his team. The outcomes produced were dramatically positive--not to mention happier and more engaged associates.

LEADING WITH LOVE

Perhaps checking in with your spirit can make the difference. As you lead others, are you communicating a spirit of openness and a genuine desire to know the other person? Are you operating from a position of love, as opposed to fear in its many ugly facets? Yes, love and compassion--both human attributes experienced from a higher connective vibration.

For is it not true that we all seek to be loved and understood?

In the corporate world, how often do leaders openly embrace foundational leadership as a demonstration of love and compassion? One corporate leader who does so is John Mackey, CEO and founder of Whole Foods. In his book, *Conscious Capitalism,* Mackey aptly advises:

"To extend our love and care beyond our narrow self-interest is antithetical to neither our human nature nor our financial success. Rather, it leads to the further fulfillment of both. Why do we not encourage this in our theories of business and economics? Why do we restrict our theories to such a pessimistic and crabby view of human nature? What are we afraid of?"

TO BE OR NOT TO BE

Perhaps two of the most profound questions posed over the course of human history are: *Who am I, and why am I here?* You may have pondered who you are as a person, a professional, a woman, a man, or a human being. "To be or not to be" leads you to fill in the blanks, but always brings you back to the ultimate question of being. Living true to your essence requires courage and honesty, qualities of great strength and integrity.

For many years I played the part of who I thought others wanted me to be: high performer, successful executive, strong male figure, breadwinner, husband and father. Years of subduing my true self brought only unhappiness and a sense of dread. I had a falseness that others would feel as an undercurrent in our interactions. When I was able to start sharing the real Michael that I am, as a unique and loving person, people around me began to have a very different experience.

As a leader, I experienced a breakthrough that allowed me to hear beyond the words of an interaction to the feelings associated with the words. This shift from autopilot to conscious awareness invited others to share openly and honestly with me. The energetic connection between me as a leader, coach, and skilled professional encouraged others to connect at a different and more human level of truth. We were cutting through barriers of fear and consequences.

Early stages of leading a new team brought with it skepticism on the part of several managers. After many months working with Priscilla, a seasoned and mature leader of thirty-two years, she confided that her initial response to my leadership was distrust. She and a few other managers had lived through many leaders managing with casual disregard for direct reports, spouting the corporate message and failing to have a genuine interest in those being led.

When I met with Priscilla over the months, I consciously opened a dialogue to understand her unique story. Instead of reacting to her ill feelings, I left my ego at the door and genuinely made every interaction about her. I invited conversation that illuminated her priorities, passions and greatest aspirations. The barriers brought forward due to her negative interactions with previous leaders began to dissipate, forming an honest professional friendship that led to accelerated performance and much greater associate engagement. Opening the door to caring for associates like Priscilla creates wonderful opportunities for shared success.

EARNING TRUST and RESPECT

I discovered that acting as "boss" is optional when being a transformative leader. Simply being "boss" in today's changing world does not automatically confer trust and respect. As leaders, we must earn the respect and loyalty of the associates we lead and serve.

I grew up as the son of an Air Force officer, a World War II B-17 pilot and war hero who, through no exercise of love and compassion, drew unquestionable respect and honor. Despite his insidious and destructive alcoholism, I accepted him as strong, decisive and powerful. Today's generation is not as quick to assign trust and undying loyalty to title alone. Rather, they seek proof through action and concrete, consistent behavior.

DISCOVERING YOUR TRUTH

To understand the power of the real you, it is imperative to know your own truth. What are you willing to stand up for in your life? Many of us wander through life never finding our true and genuine selves. We live under the illusion of truth when in fact a veil of fear covers our human experience at every level. We require ourselves to hide what we hold close inside, lest others think of us as a sham, a liar, or unlovable. Given this mindset, we often choose occupations that leave us unfulfilled and disheartened.

Intimate relationships that emerge over time fail to bring us satisfaction, for we never live from our deepest desires. We wake up middle-aged and caught in a web of dysfunction, living far below the dreams we held in our young adulthood. The gravest loss one could experience is reaching the end of our lifetime and realizing that we never stopped the cycle of fear to create a life of fulfillment, joy, and abundance.

THE REAL YOU:
Where Do You Start?

To explore what is most genuine about you, start by looking back on your early childhood, remembering the people, events, and activities that captured your enthusiasm and joy. Have you ever wondered why the exuberance expressed in young children disappears and gives way to order, obedience, and alignment?

The answer is that we are forged by society. We conform to being a good boy or girl, an obedient student regurgitating facts, and good little capitalists. Our world relegates the unique beauty of our souls to an underground space that lets in no light. This truth is tragically the product of living our lives engulfed in fear and consequent limitation. In order to break free, one must first acknowledge the unconsciousness that consumes us.

THE MAGIC OF CHILDHOOD

Like many other children, I had an imaginary friend who regularly engaged me in dialogue and childlike questions. I recall my mother asking me about my friend, urging me to move on and disassociate from him. Was this imaginary friend real or not? As an adult, can you still hear Santa's sleigh bell, as beautifully illustrated in the popular children's story, *The Polar Express*?

Do you realize that you are surrounded by infinite love, compassion and energetic connectivity urging us to align with, and be present to, our divine essence and potential?

Remember as a child those times of sheer fun and laughter, where around every turn there was something new and exciting? Remember the long summer days of play and unfiltered curiosity? Remember the creative ideas and projects that so easily and seamlessly flowed?

Where did this endless world of possibility go?

Recall your childhood, remembering the seemingly insignificant adventures, stories and excited pursuits that drew your interest and attention. I remember music stirring my soul in a powerful manner. Learning to read music, play an instrument and discover the incredible thrill of singing clearly impacted my passions. The music of the 60s, Elvis, Motown, The Beatles, the British invasion of rock n' roll artists created a psychic world of endless possibilities for my young self. Decades later and this same passion exists today, calling me to experience and participate. For the conscious leader, tapping into your childhood dreams to identify lost aspirations can lead you to discover those parts of you left dormant and hidden behind conforming attitudes, experiences and societal dictates.

YOUR INNER TRUTH

These questions are deeply relevant to all of us as leaders. All too often we are on autopilot and follow the corporate playbook. We toe the line in meting out decisions, striving to present a vision of corporate commitments, values and attributes that bring others into the fold.

The missing part of this corporate dance is our inner truth: the alignment of our leadership practices, behaviors, and attitudes to our own integrity and ethics. And your inner truth includes those early childhood passions of expression and unique personal attributes. When we operate from the external dictates of the company, absent our own unique and powerful truths, we fail those we serve and lead. We subsequently live our professional lives from a point of falseness, abstraction, and contrived allegiance. As a result, we realize unfulfilled aspirations and a life that is unbalanced.

But when you operate as a conscious leader, present and engaged in lifting up those you lead and serve, you switch on your highest self, the human being you were designed to be. Remember, this is not a dress rehearsal. Are you merely practicing to live your life or are you embracing your most powerful and luminescent self? The choice is yours to make. The real you can and will be more than what others say you are. Be courageous, be fulfilled and be the director of a joyful and meaningful life. Illuminate your ambitions to make a significant difference.

Conscious Leadership Principle #2:
BE A PEACE-BUILDER: THE INSIDE JOB!

Peace does not rest in the charters and covenants alone. It lies in the hearts and minds of all people. So let us not rest all our hopes on parchment and on paper, let us strive to build peace, a desire for peace, a willingness to work for peace in the hearts and minds of all of our people. I believe that we can. I believe the problems of human destiny are not beyond the reach of human beings.

~ John F. Kennedy

CREATING INNER PEACE

Being a conscious leader is all about connecting with other human beings. At the heart of the human connection is understanding. However, through many experiences gathered over the past several decades, I know that in order to be a great leader I must first quell the fires within my soul. Finding inner peace opens the space to create outer peace, allowing for conscious leadership to have a place to live and thrive.

For most of us, inner serenity is one of the most challenging states to achieve. But when you have built this place of peace inside you, you have mastered something powerful and precious. Because it is only from a place of peace that you can truly understand another human being.

THE FALSE SELF: EGO

For a moment, imagine planet Earth inhabited by its seven billion humans. As they walk around, their heads are down, hiding behind the scars of their experience. They are caught up in an ego-driven inner world where the incessant voice dictates a fearful existence of each person trying to hide his or her genuine self from everyone else. You know the voice to which I am referring. It's the voice that nags:

"Be careful!"
"Am I okay?"
"What if I say that?"

"Is he/she looking at me?"

"Do they know how scared I am?"

"What if they find out?"

This ego-driven false self prevents us from living where life occurs--in the present tense. Merriam Webster defines ego as, "the self, especially as contrasted with another self or the world." Sigmund Freud, in the study and practice of psychoanalysis, defines ego in relationship to three distinct parts. Id, **ego**, and super-**ego** are the three parts of the psychic apparatus defined in Freud's structural model of the psyche; they are the three theoretical constructs in terms of whose activity and interaction our mental life is described.

When we become aware of being aware, we open the door to consciousness.

REAL OF FALSE?

The distinction between the real you and your false ego self can be tricky business. Our ego keeps us within the lines, smoothing the rough edges of our emotional response and preventing us from wandering too far off the farm. Despite the appropriate controls our ego enforces, its limiting influences pull us away from living in the present tense by inserting the voice of doom, gloom, restriction, and apprehension.

Think back to when you were growing up. What did you want to do as an adult? Did you have fantasies of stardom? Did you want to dance or sing or become a doctor? Did you envision having a spouse who was your best friend, passionate lover, and soul mate?

What happened to your deepest desires? What prevented you from realizing your dreams? The answer in part lies with the limitations placed on your sense of self by a limiting ego. That ego is chiding, urging caution and removing you from the present and into the fear of an unknown future.

GAINING CONSCIOUSNESS: THE POWER OF THE BREATH

A simple way to gain access to consciousness is to breathe. Physiologically, you carry yourself, particularly in stressful or high impact moments, with very shallow breathing that stays in the upper part of the chest cavity and throat. This restrictive style of breathing fails to provide the body with life-filling air, creating a less-than-optimal framework in which to operate fully engaged in the day-to-day events of your life. Taking a moment to do a pulse-check on your breathing especially when engaged in challenging events and/or human interactions will in itself bring you to a point of increased awareness, thus allowing you to take restorative action to gain centeredness.

Take a few moments now to breathe intentionally. Feel the air flow into your lungs and fill up the chest cavity, infusing all parts of your body. Then feel the exhalation as it leaves your body, carrying with it the stress of the moment, freeing you to be present to your here-and-now experience. A few intentional breaths will almost immediately lower your heart rate, open your blood vessels and significantly reduce anxiety, stress and fear.

For those seeking a more comprehensive and durable intentional meditation and breathing exercise, the following is a seven-step mindfulness practice to incorporate into your daily life.

MINDFULNESS MEDITATION

Mindful meditation requires a purposeful intention to gain health, peace and alignment. That you would choose to be mindfully present is the first act of separating from disharmony, distraction, dis-ease and misalignment. Recognition of a deeper self, soulful and infinitely loved, becomes the mustard seed for moving toward the Divine essence we all share. Each of us is blessed with complete universal abundance of everything we need to live true to others, our infinite Divine nature and ourselves.

Yet we rarely experience this abundance because our busy lives distract us from our essence and feed chronic feelings of inadequacy, inability and scarcity. In order to contact and develop a sense of inner peace, we need to allow ourselves to step away from the daily rush of professional duties, personal commitments and relationship entanglements and invest a few minutes each day in the practice of mindfulness.

Think about it: There is no good reason not to care deeply for yourself by choosing to be mindfully present to the power of meditation. After all, if you do not take care of your body, mind and spirit, you cannot possibly realize your own potential or that of the people you lead and serve.

The investment is in two daily 15-minute exercises. This practice focuses on the exchange of the dark energy of physical, mental and spiritual blocks with the luminescence of brightly colored, restorative Divine energy. An important aspect of this practice is the intent chosen and the results desired. The question is whether you believe that the return on investment is worth the time and energy. Let us explore the investment.

Step 1: Schedule time in the morning and evening to meditate. Allocating 10 to 15 minutes will provide you with ample time to completely immerse yourself in the meditation.

Step 2: Find a comfortable place with good energy and flow. You will know this by the muted quality of outside noises (traffic, media, family conversation, etc.) Sit on a cushion or pillow, preferably on the floor, though sitting on a chair is fine, too. Perhaps you can arrange your pillow or chair in front of a window providing warm sunlight or serene scenery. The important part is to have a comfortable place to sit quietly.

Step 3: Sit with your legs crossed, back straight and head positioned straight ahead, aligned with your back and neck. Sit comfortably with your arms loose and hands at rest with the inner part of your wrists lying on your knees. Keep your hands open, fingers naturally at ease and extended.

Step 4: Gently close your eyes and do a quick body check to sense any tension and/or pressure. Wherever you find stress, mentally go to that place in your body and take several slow, deeper breaths, inhaling through your nose and exhaling through your mouth. Silently and slowly count 1, 2, 3 for both the inhale and the exhale. Continue to focus your breathing in the direction of your tension, exhaling with the mindful intention of sending your body's stress out into the universe.

Step 5: Once you have taken several intentional breaths to blow away the physical tension, shift your thoughts to bringing Divine light and energy within. As you are sitting in your meditational position, resting on the coccyx or tailbone, inhale slowly through your nose while arching your back rotating forward on the bone and allowing the back and neck to extend upward. Imagine having a straight line from your upper back through your neck and head with your nose being the end of the straight line. The head should not fall back, but rather be extended upward at a 45-degree position. As you exhale, rotate on the coccyx bone in the opposite direction having your back, neck and head rolling into a curved C with the stomach, back and head drooped forward. This pattern not only provides a natural flow through the energetic chakras, but also enlivens the senses and cleanses the spirit. In Hindu and tantric/yogic traditions and other belief systems, chakras are energy points or nodes in the subtle body.

Step 6: As you breathe, imagine exhaling the dark, chunky energy that blocks you from Divine light. See the black, brown, rust-colored toxins being exhaled through your mouth and away from your soul. As you continue to inhale while rotating forward, see the brilliant luminescent white, gold and luscious hues of the Divine enter your physical body and pulsate through you, imbuing you with love, compassion and healing. Continue the exchange until the color of your exhale is clear or bright with Divine energy. You will know that you are connected and filtering Divine essence through the crown of your head from which you can allow your deep callings and Divine essence to be totally present.

Step 7: Breathe in and be present. If your mind wanders, simply come back to the exchange of dark with light. Continue with this meditation until you experience peaceful knowing, a sense of wellness and a calming of your spirit.

INTERNAL BRUSH FIRES:
The Infernos Within

Our internal belief systems create biases that manifest as anything from pet peeves to outright barriers that block honest human exchange. We carry these certainties as unconscious screens through which all interactions are weighed and delivered.

As a leader, I recognize my own fires within, which demands intentional introspection and acknowledgment in order to quell the flames that prevent honest connection. For me, acknowledging and reconciling my own pervasive experience of abandonment, attributed to my being put up for adoption, provided important insights to address quelling the fuel-soaked nature of feeling inadequate and less-than. The subtlety and insidious nature of our smoldering internal fires can erupt into firestorms with an unintentional event or impulse brought on many times unconsciously by unintended circumstances, yet these fires within can cripple effective leadership and collaboration.

We all have our pain points--those indelible moments where love was lost, harsh circumstances found us helpless and hurt, childhood fears were never addressed--that we continue to drag along with us, as a psychic ball and chain. Unless we find healing, these firestorms continue to live on inside us and prevent us from living openly and with the freedom to be our very best selves. The task of overcoming limiting beliefs requires self-honesty and a true desire to connect with those of diverse and/or very different beliefs and opinions. The rewards are profound.

OVERCOMING LIMITING BELIEFS: Daniel

While working with a client who had accepted a new position in the desert Southwest, we were presented with some anticipated challenges. Daniel, a talented and experienced sales executive, expressed concerns in moving from a diverse and progressive urban setting to a more politically conservative and polarized part of our country. In preparation for the move and to best align a strategy that upheld his strong, politically- and socially-progressive belief system while allowing for different points of view, we collectively decided on an approach that could lead to success. The easier choice was to hold strongly to his belief system as a badge of honor, yet we realized through our work together that this position left very little room for collaboration, understanding and cooperative union. So Daniel had a plan.

Setting aside his strongly held political position, Daniel opened the door to active listening with people whose beliefs were very different from his, discovering in the process that he could find mutual ground from which to create successful synergies and outcomes.

The rewards for embracing this open and flexible approach were profound. Through the collaborative efforts, Daniel was able to realize significant dollars and support for the underserved communities he represented in his job. Even better, friendships were formed with individuals possessing divergent political ideologies and different views relating to cultural, social, economic and religious affiliations. Daniel was able to find commonalities leading to greater understanding.

From that experience, Daniel learned that as long as you seek to understand and remain consciously present, good things will grow. As a leader, it is crucial to set aside your predisposed limited beliefs--no matter how "right" they may seem to you--and to open yourself to infinite possibilities. The truth is that human beings are more alike than different.

BATTLE WITH THE MIND

Seiyu Kiriyama Kancho, spiritual leader and founder of the Agon Shu Buddhists Association, tells us that the real battle is with the mind. I have found that quieting my own mind with its incessant chattering is a goal in itself. To successfully wage war on the dark side of the mind you have many methods to employ. The best tool, described above, is intentional breathing to slow down your heart rate and provide the body, and more specifically the brain, with needed oxygen.

But there are many other ways to quiet the chatter of the mind. Among them are exercising, praying, reading a great novel, walking in nature or at the beach, listening to beautiful music, playing with your dog or cat, watching a comedy or spending intimate time with loved ones. The importance of aligning the mind to the heart cannot be underscored enough. Dis-ease and a sense of anxiety take hold whenever there is a disconnect between your heart space and your mind.

CONFRONTING INNER FEARS

The first order of business is to recognize in our humanness that these internal impediments exist. Each of us copes with his or her inner firestorms. The next step is to take action to quell the fires by getting to the root of the flames.

STOP THE SELF-CRITICISM

To find peace within, we must cease our own internal language of violence and self-deprecation. You have heard the phrase, "I am my own worst critic." Brutal self-criticism is very different from honest self-appraisal, especially when we are seeking to find a balance in our own self-perception. So often, we become consumed by how we think others see and experience us.

Many of us live our lives as chameleons, playing the role we believe others want us to play, and hiding behind a false sense of reality. How many of you have asked yourselves: How can I be liked or loved if others knew who I really was? How could I be accepted as a leader if others knew how fearful I was that I did not know everything about a topic on which I was supposed to be an expert?

It takes great strength to shed the coat of fear. To be an effective leader, it is critically important to understand fear for what it is and what it is not. Fear cannot live with love, just as darkness cannot live with light. Light can cast a shadow of darkness, but ultimately we choose whether to embrace the light or succumb to the dark side. When we discover the falsehood associated with fear, we turn on the light switch of possibility. While fear can be a powerful motivator, when left unchecked it can also infuse a state of anxiety, perpetuating a false sense of self.

ASSESSING YOUR FEARS

This two-step process begins with accurately assessing your greatest fears. Keep in mind that fears are manifested in a variety of ways, including anger, resentment, jealousy, guilt, self-righteousness, and hostility.

How do you identify what really terrifies you? One way is to reflect on your life from your earliest recollections to the present moment, and ask yourself, "What holds me back?"

UNDERSTANDING THE CONTEXT

The second step is to gain understanding of the context of your fears. Patterns can be seen in both your primary and secondary relationships. Primary relationships are based on ties of affection and personal loyalty, encompass many different aspects of our lives, and endure over long periods of time. They involve a great deal of interaction that focuses on peoples' feelings and welfare more than accomplishing specific tasks or goals. The family is a great example of primary relationships.

Secondary relationships, on the other hand, are organized around fairly narrow ranges of practical interests or goals without which the relationship would not exist. For example, the waiter-customer relationship in a restaurant is secondary because it involves a narrow range of activities (exchanging food and services for money) through which the participants meet particular needs or desires.

Take time to consider your childhood memories. Were you openly encouraged to be creative, free, and explore the world around you? Conversely, did your relationships with your parents include any clear patterns of negativity, loss, criticism, pain, or resentment? Most of us have a wide range of early experiences, both happy and challenging. Were there specific events that scarred you emotionally, experiences you have not reconciled, forgiven, or otherwise addressed appropriately? We are a composite of our life experiences. If we hold on to painful, harsh events, that baggage will manifest in our present day human exchanges, sometimes subtly and other times blatantly.

Whether others directly tell you or not, they sense your pain, feel your darkness, and want so much more from you. The very thing desired by those you lead are the human qualities you keep hidden, subdued and masked by the false smile, the sarcastic innuendo or the curt, insensitive response to an associate.

Culturally, men are taught that true masculinity means being strong, tough, unemotional and stoic. On the other hand, stereotypic roles for women, while evolving, remain undervalued in the professional world. Women who are strongly independent leaders are casually vilified and discredited. The pattern of subjugating women is not merely a part of our shared world history, but remains a toxic reality in the corporate boardrooms of today.

Understanding the context in which your fears reside clarifies and reveals the falsehood that prevents you from being fully engaged in your leadership practice let alone in all other aspects of your life. Separate the facts from the emotional toll and historical duress carried around like a monkey on your back. Shed the fears that are irrational and destructive to your honest self-expression. Are the feelings you lock inside your experiences a true manifestation of your personal and professional worth? Take the chance to expose your fears for what they are, false flags of limiting chatter!

PRUDENT RISK-TAKERS

As leaders, we strive to be prudent risk-takers. Yet where is the line between innovative and crazy? Do words of "shouldn't," "can't," and "won't" hold you back? What happens when you fail to take the risk to be more than you currently are, or ask for what you desire? You end up accepting mediocrity by failing to voice an opinion, offer a new idea, or challenge the status quo. What is the product of our failing to live fully engaged? Our limiting, ego-driven actions and behaviors lead us to resentment, anger, and regret--the byproduct of living everywhere except in the present moment of your life. Within the psychic world of resentment, anger, and regret, we live in the past. We rue our failed efforts, lack of courage, and missed possibilities associated with not following our dreams.

We can be real by understanding ourselves in our whole form. We can quiet what is latently fueled by past injuries and allow for necessary healing. It is never too late to quell the fires within. The choice is yours to make.

ACTIVE LISTENING:
Hearing Beyond the Words

How many times have you inadvertently reacted to what someone has said without taking yourself out of the issue, and been surprised or shocked by the misunderstanding that ensued?

The level of effective understanding between us is largely determined by our ability to be consciously present, not only to the words that are spoken out loud, but also to the full *intention* of the message. What is the speaker trying to convey? What is her tone of voice communicating? What are his gestures implying? What about the expression on her face, the turn of her chin, the tilt of his head?

There is so much to "listening" in every conversation.

Merriam-Webster defines the word active as "involving action or participation." Furthermore, the dictionary describes, listening as "hearing something with thoughtful attention, giving consideration." As social creatures, we spend much of our existence among others, from family to the workplace to the greater community. To find out what they really need, and what they really mean, we need to actively listen to the people in our lives.

What is passive listening? It is hearing the words without giving a damn. It means reacting to someone's comments negatively because it reminds you of your mother's chiding nature instead of hearing it correctly from the present person's mouth. Passive listening can lead to grave consequences, including poor workplace performance, broken relationships, community dysfunction, and political conflicts.

My task as a leader--and yours--is to direct communications, improve employee engagement and find creative strategies to better connect with customers.

Often what holds me back as a leader is the psychological baggage I carry as part of my collective human experience. Factors associated with my unique cultural heritage, familial accepted norms, educational advantages, and painful personal events all determine the internal wiring that affects my thoughts, actions, and aspirations.

My strong belief system can thwart effective listening by filtering the content of others' words, intentions, and behaviors. Additional complexity layers this impact when dealing with the emotions associated with the events, people, and circumstances I hold within. I have caught myself at times making a knee-jerk response to something someone said due to my strong beliefs. My job as a leader is not to change someone's belief system or alter a prejudice, but rather to listen effectively so I can support him or her in becoming a better communicator, engage effectively with employees and connect powerfully with customers.

Strong belief systems are just the outer layer of what you will need to peel away if you are going to be an effective, conscious leader. Be aware of all those auto-emotions that rise up when an event triggers a harsh memory, or people who remind you of someone else.

Yes, it is a lot to put aside, but put it aside you must in order to listen actively.

KNOW YOURSELF

In *Are You Really Listening?* Psychologists Paul Donoghue and Mary Siegel aptly point out that the most important prerequisite for being able to listen is to know ourselves, our emotions, and the psychic filters that orient our ability to listen effectively. They write: "Unless you are free to admit your emotions, to know their power, and to recognize the behaviors that these feelings compel, then their depth, their subtlety, your discomfort with them, and your ignorance of them will make listening impossible." Our filters and biases can prevent genuine listening by inaccurately or unfairly judging the intent of the communication.

The second order of active listening requires participation and the act of paying attention to the source of communication, whether that is the speaker, writer, or virtual communicator. The inherent challenges associated with active listening are well researched in the scientific community. In *How We Learn Theory*, William Glasser concludes that individuals "...learn 20 percent of what they hear, 30 percent of what they see, 50 percent of what we see and hear, 70 percent of what we discuss, 80 percent of what we experience and 95 percent of what we teach others."

Clearly, paying attention is easier said than done.

Even more complex than understanding blocks to active listening is how our brain processes information in the formulation of speech, cognitive recognition, and communication. According to research outlined in the October 16, 2009 issue of *Scientific American, Mind and Body*, Katherine Harmon details scientific data extrapolated from electrodes implanted in the Broca area of the brain, which is responsible for language. The research identified the speed at which our brain interprets and structures word sequence. The study found that "...it took about 200 milliseconds to identify a word, 320 milliseconds for grammatical composition and 450 milliseconds for phonological encoding." Phonological encoding refers to one's ability to retrieve the word's sound. It consists of two representational tiers: an ordered set of segments and a metrical representation capturing the word's syllable structure and stress pattern. (*From Wiley Online Library, Phonological Encoding of Words, Meyer & Wheeldon, 2006*)

No wonder that in the act of listening, we tend to think much faster than the speed of words being spoken. This inclination is another subtle, yet powerful detractor to active listening. In addition, cultural and environmental factors play a role in our ability to quiet the mind to afford genuine attention to listening. As you may know from experience, people from New York City tend to speak and listen at a different pace than those from other parts of the country.

NON-JUDGMENTAL LISTENING

Many powerful factors wreak havoc on our individual and collective capacity to listen non-judgmentally. The negative effects of strong judgmental factors can easily be seen in our current political malaise, as well as in our ever-widening socio-economic structures.

Internationally, for example, we see the extraordinarily complex Middle Eastern Arab-Israeli conflict that seems like an impossible amalgam of failed attempts to reconcile to peaceful coexistence. Humans have polarized opinions regarding the truth of climate change, the perilous pursuit of carbon-based fuels, the growing disparity between rich and poor, the continued subjugation of women worldwide, and numerous other critically important global concerns. This reality is indicative of our inability to set aside strong judgmental factors to truly listen and understand others. The risk here is ultimately life threatening.

So it is crucial to be open to the full intent of the message being delivered. Whether in the home, workplace, or community, we are the composite of our unique experiences with their associated emotions, as well as our relative knowledge in any given field of human endeavor. The ability to set aside these strong influences while listening will determine our success as an active listener.

To recap: Active listening is so much more than hearing words. To the extent that we seek to understand, remaining consciously present, setting aside predisposed limited beliefs, opening ourselves to possibility and remembering to exercise choice, all lead to the fundamental truth that we are more alike than different.

BEING A PEACE-BUILDER

The real you exists uncensored and unabridged, not caught up in what holds you back. The measure of your ability to live true to yourself can be found in your connections with other human beings. Think of how often you have been out shopping and salesperson says to you, "Have a nice day." Did the expression feel real or did it sound like a scripted verbal acknowledgment that the employee was instructed to say?

ARE YOU GENUINE?

What about you? When you interact with a colleague or friend, do you have a genuine desire to know if the other person is doing well when you say, "How's it going?" And how does the other person know that you really care? You know the difference: When someone asks you how you're doing--and means it--you experience the energy of his or her warm consideration.

WAKING UP

Take notice in your day of how many people are actually awake, conscious, and living in the present moment. It may take you some time to identify a person living in this manner. When you do find such a person, notice how you feel their sincerity. What visceral feeling do you receive? There is a clear contrast in those interactions with people who are awake, genuinely care, and are interested. You witness non-verbal presence including direct eye contact, an attentive body language inviting you to participate, and an energetic connection of invisible yet palpably infused sharing.

Now, shift this awareness to yourself. How are you engaging those who you lead? Are you consciously being real or are you following the corporate playbook, pasting on a smile and parroting what you are told to say?

Living true to your real you means keeping the chatterbox ego in check and quelling the fires that prevent authentic human connection. Seeking and finding inner peace is a prerequisite to building peace externally. Take the risk to be yourself in your highest aspiration.

The real you lives fully and vibrantly in the here-and-now, not in the fear of an unknown future or the regret of an unrealized past.

Conscious Leadership Principle #3:
BE PRESENT

If your mind carries a heavy burden of past, you will experience more of the same. The past perpetuates itself through lack of presence. The quality of your consciousness at this moment is what shapes the future.

~Eckhart Tolle

A FINE BALANCE

Effective leadership requires strategic planning and preparation for determining a profitable future. At the same time, as a leader, you need to live fully in the present. Does this seem counterintuitive? How can you strike a healthy balance between the necessity of planning and the power of wholly living present for those we serve and lead?

Not unlike the quantum physics theory that posits our ability to simultaneously exist in multiple locations across time and space, we do have the exquisite capacity to see an uncertain future---which includes a myriad of unknown variables from market conditions to international trade---and still remain present with those we lead. The idea that we are limited to a singular structured existence fails to consider that we are more than our physical forms.

We know that our intellectual output represents only a fraction of our potential. We also know that in our human form we are a balance between body, mind, and spirit. Holistic thinker Edgar Cayce introduced this concept as the "triune self."

CAUSE AND EFFECT

Our actions are largely the product of personal choices that dictate the course of our lives. And unless we are living as hermits, our behavior impacts those around us, either directly or indirectly. Cause and effect play out as we make choices in our execution of leadership. The differentiating factor is the degree to which we choose to live consciously present in the world around us. Let us not minimize the effect our energetic and spirited selves bring to those we lead.

THE ENERGY MANAGER

In many ways, we are "energy managers." As human beings, we are electrically wired as very specialized and unique electromagnetic, super-conducting, holistic spiritual entities. In simpler terms, we exist as *energized* human beings.

RAMPING UP OUR ENERGY FIELD

Just as we know that water conducts electricity, our bodies are primarily constructed of liquid. While we may not have the ability to see the energetic output of our electric fields, is there any question as to the flow of energy that exists between human beings? Why are we attracted to some people and not to others?

Have your ever been in a large gathering of people--a cocktail party, for instance--and turned suddenly to watch a man or woman enter the room? You are drawn to his or her presence as you witness others also turning to notice this person. Why is it that you turned and focused attention on this individual as opposed to others entering the gathering? What is it about this person that compelled your energetic attention? Sure, it could be what they are wearing or their physical appearance, but there is more than what appears on the surface. We are attracted to this person because their energy field is powerful and visceral.

Living in the present tense opens the door to conscious decision-making. We can make choices about our thoughts, intentions, and actions. When orchestrated from a point of love and compassion, these choices offer others a much higher vibration.

ATTUNING TO HIGHER VIBRATIONS

We live in a world of three dimensions, a construct that forms substance to provide context for what we perceive and experience as life. But there are higher orders, higher dimensions that, while not visible to our human form, exist nonetheless.

Take love and compassion. Can you touch love? Throughout our human story, masters of music, art and literature have provided physical form to honor and signify love--a poem, a beautiful ballad, a rich and lush novel or the paintings of the Renaissance, to name a few. And while it may be challenging to provide concrete physical form to higher levels of order, as sensitive entities we are quick to feel the passions of love, feel the anguish of loss, feel the sensation of compassion and feel the attraction that some elicit from us.

Do these feelings exist or are we falsely constructing something that without form does not exist at all? Deep questions, but relevant in the context of higher vibrations.

TUNING UP YOUR HIGHER SELF

Ever heard someone say, "I'm in the groove" or "on the path?" For conscious leaders, we are on the path when we let go of that which constrains us, those confining elements of time, space and restrictively narrow and limiting voices. Remove the barriers to honest and genuine human connection and tune up your higher self.

As a visually oriented learner, I imagine myself in a small wooden boat on a stream flowing serenely along a beautifully wooded and grassy scene. I have with me in the boat one oar to employ for guiding the small craft as it winds through the curves of the stream. Up ahead are what appear to be rapids, churning and accelerating the velocity of the water. One choice is to grab the oar and make a beeline to a fork in the stream that appears to be calmer. Do I choose to steer the boat in a different direction or do I stay the course?

The options lead to very different outcomes, as do the choices we make in how we lead those we serve. After steering my boat to what appear to be easier, less stressful paths, as I have done many times in my life, I realize that what I could not have seen were the dangerous waterfalls ahead. The higher vibrations associated with being aware and conscious guide us to stay on a higher course, aligning to our higher selves. When we allow ourselves to be present, we are aligning to our true nature, that of caring and supporting the best in others. The energetic ripple is visceral and connective.

MAGNETIC STRENGTH

Consider for a moment that the magnetic strength of our being is predicated on the intensity and level of presence we are engaging in at any particular moment in time. Therefore, choosing to be present in our thoughts and intentions creates a flow of energy very different than the level exhibited when operating on autopilot. Conscious leadership requires having the eyes to see and the ears to hear, but most importantly, the quality of being present.

NEGATIVE vs. POSITIVE RESPONSES

The question has risen repeatedly over my lifetime of whether we, as human beings, are predisposed to choose a negative response over a positive one. The millennia of human history shows an endless series of male-dominated, female-subjugated, violent, and aggressive chapters. This history clearly demonstrates that the human family is wracked by negativity, control, power, money, and war. Our recent history has revealed the cancerous greed bred by those in power who continue to want more at the expense of all others. The financial collapse of 2008-2009 and the subsequent worldwide recession paint a picture of a world out of control, spiraling down the rabbit hole of dark energy.

Can one person make a difference in a world controlled by forces beyond our direct impact? The answer is definitive: *yes.*

HARNESSING and MANAGING ENERGY

Over the past decade, I have come to experience the power of living presently and choosing my energetic output. Several years ago while collaborating to build a retail bank sales culture, I realized that effective leaders are in fact best described as "Energy Managers." So when asked what I did for a living, I would respond that what I did was manage others' energies.

Inevitably my answer would prompt a curious question, "What do you mean, manage others' energies?" To which I would reply, "We all are endowed with the capacity to energetically produce."

Harnessing the collective energies of those you lead ultimately determines the quality and quantity of the work they undertake. It is important to create an environment where others feel free to be energized, which enlivens their lives in ways otherwise not realized. The environment you create encourages participation with strong respect and uncompromised honor for those you lead. Your own energy becomes the model for others to follow. Upbeat, confident, inclusive and consistent describe the internal energy necessary to foster an optimal work environment. To witness others turned on energetically not only creates much higher productivity but taps into individual passions. When focused to the greater whole, that passion inevitably raises the quality of results. This in turn can measurably improve the quality of participants' lives, not to mention increased employee engagement, customer satisfaction and profits.

REALIZING YOUR OWN POWER

As an energy manager, your power cannot be underscored enough. Work with it! Play with it! Find ways in which you can become more aware of it. For example, I would experiment by occasionally choosing to enter my workplace taking on a negative angry affect. Without saying a word, I noticed those around me picking up on my aura of disgruntlement. The dark energy permeated the environment as a shadow of storm clouds diffusing the sunlit skies in preparation for a thunderous downpour.

In witnessing this pall of negativity sweep through the collective energy of my colleagues, I would choose then to break the force by engaging one of my associates from a position of love, care, and humor. Immediately the clouds parted and the energetic field lightened measurably. Over and over again I experimented with this process and found a similar sequence of events. The perpetual business demand for better, bigger, faster, cheaper and more innovative leads us to gloss over the energetic power we possess. Yes, *what* we do is important. But *how* we do what we do is the difference between just plain good and extraordinary.

When you choose to be fully present, you are able to realize the full extent of your personal energetic power.

CHOOSE YOUR BATTLES

While you may not have a direct impact on how others make their choices and live their lives, you do have the ability to protect your own serenity and peace of mind by choosing *not* to engage where appropriate. Sometimes the greatest action to take is no action at all. Pick your battles carefully.

Ask yourself the following questions:

- Do I need to be right?
- Is the issue or challenge a boulder as opposed to a pebble on the beach?
- Will my integrity be negatively impacted?

- Am I able to act with love, compassion, and understanding?

If the answer to any or all of these questions is affirmative, then by all means go ahead and engage. If not, perhaps the best response is no response at all.

THE COLLECTIVE UNCONSCIOUSNESS

When you elevate the energetic flow that enlivens and invites others to join, the *ripple effect* includes expressions of love, compassion, and understanding. This in turn, leads to feelings of happiness, both in others and in ourselves. We can engage those we serve to better realize their unique powerful selves, thus energetically elevating them.

WE ARE ALL CONNECTED

The term "collective unconsciousness," as coined by Carl Jung, father of analytical psychology, proposes that it is part of the *unconscious* mind, expressed in humanity and all life forms with nervous systems, and describes how the structure of the psyche autonomously organizes experience. So our capacity for creating change does not stop at the individual layer, but impacts a greater whole. What we do in any given moment, as the product of our thoughts and intentions, acts to create a unifying effect across the collective unconsciousness. It really does matter what happens to other people; we all can feel it. Whether the sufferer is a drone victim or starving child or a friend in need, all suffering sends a wave of despair across the collective unconsciousness. As does joy.

When we act from our true and authentic selves, we align to the higher order frequency of love and understanding. Our act sends a positive vibrational wave through humanity. The differences we experience among others are only iterations of the same humanness we all share. We each experience passion, grief, loss, hunger and desire. As citizens of the planet, we all belong to a shared humanity.

Every action you take as a leader has an impact, not just in the workplace, but across the entire human family. Every time you choose to be open and real with those you lead and serve, the impact is exponential. When your associates feel empowered to realize their greatest aspirations, they walk with a different energy. By becoming conscious leaders, you can support others to be better, not just in the workplace but also in the home, the community, and the global collective. They become better friends, spouses, partners, and human beings.

Everyone you touch benefits from your shift. Empowering others to be true to themselves catalyzes a move from fear to love, from apathy to active participation, from separateness to unity.

LIMITS TO OUR CONTROL

Events in life cannot always be controlled. But you can control your present state of mind. Whether you choose to react as a victim or respond with acceptance and compassion, you can define the direction your life takes by choosing the high road.

I think of the many times over the years when I was tasked with terminating an employee for acts of impropriety, ethics violations, theft, and other serious corporate infractions. One does not become good at firing employees--at least those of us with a heart. Yet, there have been occasions when the very best action for the employee was to end their misery in working for the company. When I approached the task with this belief, that it was for their highest good, any unpleasantness shifted into acceptance and even optimism on their part.

CHOOSING POSITIVITY

In your personal life, choose to surround yourself with others who are awake, conscious, and living their lives from a place of love and understanding. In your professional capacities, try fostering an environment where others demonstrate a strong propensity to contribute in a positive manner.

Do not let discouragement infiltrate your spirit if this approach does not always work out. Not all humans are ready to wake up. Be present to the fact that an associate is disgruntled or disengaged. Notice associates who do not respond to your positivity.

Great leaders demonstrate a strong presence of accountability, a responsibility to lead others up, or manage them out. Your compassion lies in the understanding that some individuals are incapable of making the hard choices associated with taking control of their own destinies.

INTUITIVE POPS

In my professional coaching, I have learned to be present to what I call "intuitive pops." These are flashes of energetic impulse prompting me to stop and take notice. This level of awareness can be cultivated, the more you live consciously.

INTUITIVE POPS IN ACTION

In my role as bank executive, as part of our corporate performance management process, I met individually with my managers to provide them with a quarterly performance review along with a development plan. While I have performed these types of reviews for many years, this round was very different. These meetings were infused with an intentional presence that led to remarkable dialogue and profound opportunities, not just for me but also for those bank managers I serve.

With 15 performance reviews to accomplish over a three-day period, managing my time was critically important. Yet, I did so with a purposeful allotment of time in order to have meaningful reviews. By 3 pm on day one of my schedule, I had met with four managers. Number five was with Joan, a successful leader who has shown noticeable improvement in her performance over the past several months. After reviewing the standard areas of performance and discussing professional development opportunities, I prepared to move on to the last review of a long day. Joan stopped me as I was walking toward the door.

Her voice suddenly was more emotional and genuine as she said, "Michael, what is the one thing I need to do in order to be a better leader?"

I have learned to pay close attention to intuitive pops that jar my spirit and this was one of them. I turned, smiled, and said, "Sit down, let's talk some more." The student arrives when the master is ready.

As though I unconsciously flipped an energy switch, I immediately turned on and was available in a much different way to Joan. Without hesitation, I was catapulted into an elevated state of awareness, feeling the electric soulful impulse to shift.

"Tell me what you believe is your greatest opportunity," I asked.

Thoughtfully, yet with a sense of great frustration and agitation, she began telling me how disappointed she was in not being able to achieve higher performance, attributing much of the blame on her two direct report leaders. "I should put the entire team on performance management discipline," she concluded.

My attention to Joan was visceral, energetic, and without judgment. I simply listened with full attention, not interrupting or thinking of what I would say next. I then asked her to separate for a moment from the bank.

"Visualize with me that you are a highly skilled surgeon who is paid to remove cancerous tissue from your patients," I said. Quickly and easily, she moved into the visualization with me. "Now, I want you to elevate yourself to another level, to that of healer. As a healer and a surgeon, you care for the whole self -- body, mind, and spirit. Your interest is in healing the entire person." Joan's eyes portrayed understanding.

I continued by telling her that the body was her entire banking center team. "How would you care for the whole person as a healer, Joan?"

She thought for a moment and said, "I would make sure they had enough good food, exercise, and rest."

"Yes!" I exclaimed. "What else would you do?"

I felt an opening of her energy as she quietly responded, "I would care for them."

"And remember as a surgeon, your skill is necessary in cutting away that which is diseased," I said. "Taking your frustration and disappointment out on your entire team would be like surgically removing the head due to an earache. Now would that make sense?"

Her smile illuminated our dialogue as she nodded in agreement.

"How do you feel right now?" I asked.

"I feel much lighter," she said.

I then asked her to remember the feeling. I went on to tell her that her appearance had changed as a result of getting to the heart of her discontent. The darkness in her eyes had dissipated, as had the tension in her smile. Streams of lightness had taken the place of her internal conflict. She had shared with me her struggle, opening up about the baggage she carried around. She had been authentic.

"Your greatest leadership opportunity is in caring for and expressing love and compassion to those you lead and serve," I told her. "As a surgeon there are times when you must surgically remove the disease that, if left unchecked, will take down the entire team."

As we stood to say goodbye, I could see that Joan was sparkling with aliveness. The customary polite, rote handshake seemed inappropriate and out of context. Joan and I shared a caring hug. Pulling away from her, a tear glimmered on her cheek, adorning her radiant smile.

This level of awareness can be honed by choosing to become consciously aware of what is going on around you. By operating with your intuitive lights on, you allow for alternative, and truthful, ways of knowing.

Listen beyond the words that are spoken, and instead hear what is being said from a desire to understand. Trust that unexpected voice inside you that says, "go left," when you think you are supposed to turn right!

PRACTICE LISTENING TO YOUR INTUITION

There are several ways to improve your ability to hear your intuition. The first method is to tune into your body. At any given moment in time during your daily interactions, stop and ask yourself, "How am I feeling?" Where do I feel stress, tension and/or pain? It might be in your stomach, with a feeling of dis-ease and perhaps even slight nausea. Or you may feel your neck and shoulders aching with tightness. Identifying areas in your body that are not in alignment with a calm and centered state of being are clues to something in your situation that you need to pay attention to, and/or a misalignment to your truths.

Another way to increase your awareness of intuition is to pay attention to your senses, to your observations and to your basic wits. Discerning between intuition and wishful thinking or fear requires practice. When you are present you have a much greater ability to hear your inner voice, that GPS guidance system that can alert you to falseness and/or a healthier direction to choose.

Taking practice a bit further, experiment with your intuition on small things. For instance, step outside your house or place of business and choose a direction to walk based on the guidance of your inner voice. See what happens as a result of your choice. Being attuned to your intuition can provide you with valuable insight and support as you undertake your leadership responsibilities.

BEING FULLY PRESENT

In simple terms, being present leads to more happiness, which leads to more success.

Each of us has a choice. We can choose to be the sentinel of the corporate playbook, following all the rules and managing employees from a position of authority. Or we can choose to be fully present to what is needed in the moment, and lead employees from a position of intuitive understanding. Opting for the second way brings out the very best in us as well as those we lead and serve. We become the energy manager necessary to harness the collective potential of those we lead.

THE IMPACT ON YOU

The personal impact of leading others from a state of presence is profound. Gaining a holistic perspective in your leadership methodology means lifting yourself up to a higher plateau, a richer life experience. When you become more present with those you lead, the connection enlivens to embrace a fuller, more meaningful interaction encouraging honesty and genuine authenticity. In this elevated exchange there exists a deeper sense of caring and understanding. When you choose to operate from a conscious level, your life changes in ways that add health and happiness to your experience.

Choosing to live in the present tense quiets the voice of the ego, curtailing the incessant chatter that pulls you into the past or a fearful future.

THE IMPACT ON OTHERS

There is a greater sense of purpose as well as a calmness that results when you are present to those you lead and serve. By lifting others up, your gain is exponential.

When others feel your intentional openness and willingness to understand their struggles and aspirations, the opportunity for shared success grows immensely.

Not only is this highly beneficial to those we serve, but it also infuses the organization with employees who are more engaged, empowered, and happier. Your customers can see and feel this change, and by the very nature of attraction, they become more apt to do business with you.

The practical implications of leading others from a point of consciousness are profound. Happy customers spend more, grow their business, and tell their friends.

So, leading consciously from a place of being fully in the present moment, *does* ensure a positive, forward-thinking future.

Conscious Leadership Principle #4:
BE A RISK-TAKER!

But he'd learned long ago that a life lived without risks pretty much wasn't worth living. Life rewarded courage, even when that first step was taken neck-deep in fear.
~ Tamera Alexander

Risk taking is an essential part of effective leadership. As a leader, you must take risks in many areas of your professional life, as you do in your personal world. Success is not for the faint of heart but for those who are willing to be courageous, take prudent chances and dare to step into the adventure of the unknown. The courage separating conscious leaders from the rest is expressed in the resolve to stand in the heat of debate when others give up or run.

Equally significant to successful risk-takers is their ability to inspire others by envisioning outcomes that others simply cannot see. Taking the chance to give an associate, who possesses the talent but lacks the experience, the opportunity to lead a project and/or champion a part of your business can have multiplying positive benefits. Your tenacious ability to stand up for what you truly believe in spite of your belief being unpopular, or having the strength to hold yourself to the kind of integrity that builds trust are qualities that mark a conscious leader willing to take on risk.

RISK TAKERS COME IN MANY FORMS

We all know the stories of corporate giants who took a chance to follow their dreams and passions. We are familiar with such titans as Henry Ford, Thomas Edison, and Steve Jobs for their unrelenting commitment to pursuing their callings.

But do we also consider others, not associated with corporate America, such as Martin Luther King, Jr., John F. Kennedy, Gandhi, Nelson Mandela, Eleanor Roosevelt, Susan B. Anthony and Rosa Parks for their courage to stand up against tyranny, the status quo, persecution, and hatred?

Whether in the boardrooms of Ford, GE, or Apple, or in the fight against oppression, these individuals were pillars of strength. Naysayers, violent attacks, imprisonment and outright hatred did not sway them. They represent a breed of leader willing to take a risk for more.

As a leader, what are *you* willing to stand for?
Do you consider yourself a risk-taker?
Do you have the courage and strength to stand up to those who say, "Not possible"?
Are you willing to pursue what you believe is true?

A CONTEMPORARY RISK-TAKER: Elon Musk

To pursue what we believe is true, we must wake up from the illusions of limitations and impossibility. One contemporary visionary leader who has challenged the paradigm of limitations is Elon Musk. Not only has he successfully built an empire taking on the carbon-based automobile industry with his Tesla electric vehicles, but also set his sight of tackling the cosmos with his SpaceX program.

Musk epitomizes a human being who did not abandon his childhood passions. Growing up, space travel and exploration fueled his interests. Astronaut Neil Armstrong was his idol, representing a man of courage and unrelenting vision. Despite his continued reverence for the first man on the moon, when Armstrong criticized Musk's desire to commercialize space via his SpaceX program, he was not dissuaded in the least. Rather than acquiesce to naysayers, Musk continues to embrace an expanded intelligence to push the envelope of science and the status quo corporate construct to ask a basic question: *Why not?*

There are others doing extraordinary work on the planet, but their numbers are relatively few. Conscious leadership demands risk-taking as a guiding principle, for to do anything less relegates you to the status of follower. Dare to dream, take a stand on your dreams, and be the leader who asks, "Why not?"

CAPITALISM:
A System of Control

Imagine for a moment that our world did not operate from the ever-present psychic and emotional reality of scarcity. Can you picture a world in which we all had enough of what we need to survive and thrive as a global family?

"That's science fiction," you may say. Is it? Let us take a closer look.

ILLUSION OF CONTROL

In the capitalist model, we cede our economic control to others. We are allowed to play in this market, but ultimate control rests with those who possess the capital.

Merriam-Webster defines capitalism as, "an economic system characterized by private or corporate ownership of capital goods, by investments that are determined by private decision, and by prices, production, and the distribution of goods that are determined mainly by competition in a free market."

In the current paradigm of the privatization of control, those who actively participate gain resources and the advantages of wealth. Are we then surprised that those who do not participate are left with the reality of scarcity? For the majority of people in the United States, equal access is a fallacy parading as an aspiration, advertised by those who control as the ultimate goal.

Yet, the truth is that planet Earth possesses everything the human population needs, thus eliminating the current reality of scarcity. We define our reality by what we perceive, for in the presence of perception we form our views of the world and our place in it.

THE ROOTS OF GREED

There is no doubt that a driving force behind the financial collapse of 2008/2009 was due to corporate greed and the ruthlessly criminal and corrupt practices of those in power. Yet is greed the root of our disparity? Charles Eisenstein, author of *Sacred Economics*, offers a compelling thesis that greed is not the root, but rather a symptom of the perception of scarcity. So what is the root of this notion of scarcity? Eisenstein contends that:

> "Greed makes sense in a context of scarcity. Our reigning ideology assumes it: it is built in to our Story of Self. The separate self in a universe governed by hostile or indifferent forces is always at the edge of extinction, and secure only to the extent that it can control these forces."

And the ultimate control of our existence then becomes that of a world perpetuating the illusion of separateness.

Our way of life centers on this structural concept--winners vs. losers, strong vs. weak and haves vs. have-nots. Certainly, greed is a pervasive element that calls into question individual and corporate integrity, but in truth, our planet is bounding with abundance. What's the issue, you ask? Eisenstein goes on to say,

"So immersed in scarcity are we that we take it to be the nature of reality. But in fact, we live in a world of abundance. The omnipresent scarcity we experience is an artifact: of our money system, of our politics, and of our perceptions."

Our notion of scarcity is a man-made phenomenon, created by a monetary system that supports our capitalist model, pitting one person and/or one organization against the other in a win-lose scenario. This plays out on the international stage as well among sovereign nations warring to acquire land, oil and other valuable resources. Those who control the money, control the resources, including natural resources, energy resources, and human resources. Those in control seek to protect their interests by directly and indirectly precluding others from entering into the system by preventing upward mobility and turning aside legislative policies of fairness and equality, all orchestrated to amass more and more.

TRANSFORMATION *IS* POSSIBLE

Does your belief system allow room for considering that transformation is possible? The win-lose competitive structure of capitalism has insidiously infused itself into our cultural psyche. This phenomenon is not just apparent in our corporate construct, but is inherent in all aspects of our society. You can see its footprint from the educational system to the spoils of a divorce court, from the contemporary version of gladiator warfare on the gridiron to the political debates of climate change, immigration reform, gun control, and oil drilling. Winners take all--or as much as they can--is our driving philosophy.

Leaders, are you willing to take the risk of consciously transforming an old view of capitalism into one that is inclusive, cooperative and collaborative?

THE POWER OF CHARISMA

Have you ever had the experience of being in a large audience and hearing a passionate leader share his/her visionary message? There may have been several hundred people in the audience, but you felt as though the speaker was talking directly to you. You felt it; you experienced the message viscerally as if you were the only person in the hall.

What is it that this amazing speaker was able to convey to the audience that connected with you so profoundly? The words were important, but the emotional resonance--which you experienced energetically--made the difference in how you received the message. In short, you felt the speaker's charisma.

In an increasingly apathetic and dulled-down world order, breaking free of mediocrity and status quo demands consciousness. In a conscious state, opportunities exist to choose differently, options that consider all the moving parts of the whole. Being a conscious leader requires that your internal mechanisms are functioning with balance. As much as cognitive intelligence is a favorable human commodity, it pales in relation to the importance of leading from the heart. Freedom from that which holds you back necessitates trusting your intuition and seeing with eyes that are visionary.

Leaders embrace their passions with an intensity that propels them forward, unafraid to challenge the status quo, and inviting others to join in their excitement. Great leaders all possess the attribute of charisma: a special charm or appeal that causes people to feel attracted and excited by someone. They have an energetic output that beckons others to listen, observe, and participate.

We are drawn to those leaders who capture our longings, embodying our truths and deepest aspirations. Conscious leaders understand the responsibility that comes with coalescing the spirits and passions of those they lead.

Our history has shown the negative sides to charismatic leaders who use their powerful skills to manipulate and propagate a hierarchy of separation, a movement of control, power and grave atrocities. Adolph Hitler's rise to power in the 1930s is one poignant example. There are others throughout our short human history.

Yet we have beautiful examples of charismatic leaders who recognized their special skills in bringing about significant change directed at falsifying the notion of separate and apart. Leaders such as Nelson Mandela, Martin Luther King and Gandhi raised our hearts and minds to wage war against oppression, hatred and racism. Rosa Parks, in her singular yet powerful statement of courage--refusing to move to the back of a public bus--took on a culture of blatant discrimination and racial separation ultimately leading to the Civil Rights movement. They were brave enough to challenge the status quo and elevate our human experience.

So many leaders, though, stand back, keep their mouths shut, and tow the company line without questioning the authority of their direct report managers, even when the style of leadership is offensive and toxic. In fact, I have witnessed grown men break down in tears over their manager publicly chastising them for lack of performance. I have been in corporate meetings where the directives being given were harshly negative and leveraged, as a tool for ultimately downsizing unwanted associates. This style of managing others is anything but conscious leadership, for it minimizes, degrades and creates a culture of fear.

One may argue whether charisma can be learned or not, that it simply is a characteristic with which someone is born. My experience working with associates and clients has shown dramatic outcomes with leaders attempting to improve their charismatic connection. The freedom to be fully engaged in a charismatic fashion demands the courage to take on the risk of being real, of leading from a point of truth and honesty as well as seizing the opportunities to connect powerfully with those you lead.

EXPANDING YOUR CHARISMA

Jasmine, a mid-level executive in a Fortune 500 company, came to me looking to enrich her leadership abilities. "How can I be more persuasive and charismatic?" she asked. "My team does not give me their full attention during meetings. They seem distracted and are more interested in their email than in listening to me."

I inquired, "When you think of a charismatic leader, who comes to mind?"

Without hesitation, she responded, "Martin Luther King."

I smiled and nodded in agreement. "Yes, Dr. King was an incredibly charismatic figure." After a moment of silence, I asked: "Why do you think he was so magnetic?"

Jasmine replied, "There was something about his ability to speak with authority, a confidence he exuded, almost a deep conviction that what he was saying was truth! He seemed to speak a truth that so many longed for."

"What else?" I prodded.

Thoughtfully, Jasmine said, "He was passionate about what he spoke about. And he seemed to listen intently when others were sharing with him."

"Exactly," I affirmed.

Brainstorming together, we continued to discuss what it takes to be charismatic: a confident voice, direct eye contact, listening with intense interest, a firm tone and above all else, authentic passion. Yes, passion! It permeates others when expressed with strong presence and conviction. And I reminded Jasmine to not forget the amazing power of a genuine smile.

For her team, Jasmine decided to modify her leadership behaviors to include these attributes. She also made it a point to bring her associates into the dialogue, inviting them to share their opinions and thoughts on how to carry out the work at hand.

We practiced voice intonation and the importance of delivering her words with confidence and passion. Over the next several weeks, Jasmine made significant improvement in developing a charismatic leadership style. Her team responded favorably and the overall quality and quantity of work improved greatly.

INTEGRITY AND ETHICS

PROFITS vs. WELLBEING

How many leaders work in organizations that systematically put profits and revenue ahead of associate wellbeing and inclusion? Do we stand by silently and turn a blind eye lest we be cast as a renegade or troublemaker?

We have created a corporate culture of fear, where standing up for personal integrity or demanding accountability for scrupulous business practices is a dangerous undertaking. Fear of job loss, being classified as a naysayer and/or facing the wrath of superiors are just some of the threats that prevent honest and appropriate debate, dialogue and reevaluation.

RISK TAKING A STAND

We have an epidemic of unethical practices in our country, evidenced by the financial crisis that left hundreds of thousands of families foreclosing on their homes and massive job loss. As a society, we have come to accept that corporations can get away with massive theft, lying and corruption.

Who takes the risk to stand up for what is right? Is it necessary that conscious leaders leave corrupt and misleading companies? Perhaps it is. But maybe the answer lies in having the courage to question the norms, push for reform, and demand ethical decision-making.

Profits and ethics can live in the same room.

RISK CARING FOR OTHERS

Conscious leadership invites you to take the extra moment to actually care about those you lead and learn about them beyond the formalities of business protocol. Connecting emotionally and establishing a foundational relationship with your associates is not to pry into their private lives, but rather to let them know you care for them. You can demonstrate that you are engaged in knowing their aspirations. You thus become intentional in your desire to lead them effectively.

Leadership is a human enterprise. The choice is yours as to whether you are willing to take the risk of being genuinely interested in your direct employees beyond the reporting structures in place.

The payoff is forging emotional connections that provide greater associate engagement, motivated team members willing to exert that extra degree of effort, and ultimately better customer satisfaction leading to greater profits.

CONNECTING TO A VISION

Being a visionary is worthless unless others align themselves to follow your vision. We all have many concepts, plans and dreams. Bringing those great ideas to fruition by developing strategies, plans and structures is critical to your success. Believing in your ability as a leader is risky business. But having a vision demands thoughtful and purposeful leadership.

MAKING YOUR VISION A REALITY

An integral part of being able to realize our visions is to invite those we lead and serve to join us. Yes, *invite* them!

When our vision becomes more about satisfying our own need for self-aggrandizement or control, others sense this and are reticent to follow. Conversely, when your vision includes those you lead in the fruits of your labor and subsequent success, you lift up everyone around you to share in the rewards. And while your ideas may have great potential, they pale when measured against diverse and collective inclusion of those being led.

TRUST AND RESPECT

In today's fast-paced world, respect and trust are not earned simply by title. Leaders must be willing to work by establishing the loyalty and trust of those they serve through their actions, behaviors, and personal connections made with each and every associate.

Dare to dream! Dare to inspire! Being brave is risky business. So, too, is standing up for your beliefs or for a friend or associate. But ultimately, such risk-taking is worth the effort. Courage is exactly what will make you stand out in a crowd. It is how people will recognize you as a conscious leader.

Conscious Leadership Principle #5:
BE A TRANSFORMATIVE COMMUNICATOR

You can talk with someone for years, everyday, and still, it won't mean as much as what you can have when you sit in front of someone, not saying a word, yet you feel that person with your heart, you feel like you have known the person for forever.... connections are made with the heart, not the tongue.

*   ~ C. JoyBell*

Communication is much more than words. The word communication derives from the Latin word for "share." When you share something, it is not just meted out, it is received. There is a give and take.

But in our world, we tend to think of "communication" as merely conveying information. The truth is, no matter how many memos, letters, emails or voicemail messages you send out, if they are not read or heard, there is no communication. Employee surveys distributed annually by companies show a perpetually clear message that communication is always a challenge.

Many years ago, I worked in the telecommunications industry where it was prophesized that technological advances would revolutionize corporate communications. It never occurred. Why? Because to be an effective communicator, you need to create an environment where your message matters and is fully received.

The "how" of communication---in this case, technology---does not matter nearly as much as the "what" of communication. And for you, as a conscious leader, the "what" needs to be the human connection.

THE TECHNOLOGY REVOLUTION

It is hard to believe that the Internet is only twenty-five years old. Its ubiquitous presence is linked to nearly every aspect of our lives. It is remarkable to witness the dramatic impact of this technology in the span of one generation. The motor skills of today's children seem to be imbued with the innate ability to operate flawlessly in this technology.

Equally entwined in our culture is the communication advances experienced in the corporate mainstream with the emergence of online companies. Consumer behavior has been transformed by the Internet on all fronts, from online banking to shopping to dating and beyond. These technological advances have hugely impacted all elements of our society.

Yet the field of leadership, operating in a world of cyber real-time communications, presents both unique opportunities and challenges in our ability to connect as human beings.

SOCIAL MEDIA

I find it both interesting and worrisome that so many people describe friendship by the number of Facebook friends on their profile, when they have never met face-to-face or even exchanged words with many of these individuals. The very nature of our cyber world has created a platform on which interpersonal relationships are defined not by the intimacy of human exchange, but rather from an impersonal connection on a social media website. Meeting in cyberspace allows for individuals to be who they want to be, leaving behind both personality flaws and uniquely precious parts of their essence. Perhaps the question is: How lonely do you feel amidst all this connectivity?

Increasingly, intimacy in the form of real, heart-to-heart encounters is a casualty of our new world order.

INTIMACY-THE REAL CONNECTION

In 1976, as part of my undergraduate degree program at Syracuse University, I took advantage of studying abroad in Strasbourg, France. My International Relations degree program brought me to an impassioned pursuit of the protection of human rights. Strasbourg was an ideal place of study since the Court and Commission of Human Rights, as part of the Council of Europe structure formed after World War II, was housed in this historic city on the Rhine. At 21, I thought of myself as an adventurous, forward-thinking young man, filled with passionate ideas and ready to show the French how openly progressive my thinking and behavior was in acculturating into their way of life. After all, I believed Americans were leaders in counter-culture movements with women's liberation, music, literature and civil rights at the forefront.

It did not take long for me to realize that I was a neophyte when it came to intimacy and true liberation. I had never experienced the friendship and intimacy shared with a group of students over hours of deep and expressive dialogue, sitting together in cafes, drinking espresso in the mornings and beer or wine in the afternoons as we talked about French politics, international affairs, cultural differences, gender identification and even sensitive issues of sex, drugs and of course, rock n' roll. This level of interpersonal communications took me deeper into learning about others, getting to know them beyond a casual hello and beginning to understand their joys, losses and aspirations.

Returning home, landing at JFK Airport in New York, I recall my eyes welling with tears, regret and an indelible imprint of the true nature of intimacy and friendship.

Fast forward to the present day global community brought together through the expansive connectivity of the Internet. My French experience demonstrated the power of the human connection when finding the time to actually care enough about others to seek understanding and commonality. Transformative communication demands connecting beyond the words of an email or text message. Intimacy among people requires more than friends on Facebook or the drill Sargent approach to doling out directives and/or coaching to filling out forms or smart plans. Yet, let us not dismiss the incredibly powerful capacity of our global worldwide web.

The advances of our technological communications have been the key to triggering historically significant movements such as the Arab Spring or Occupy Wall Street. These are just some of the outcomes, as well as so many breakthrough scientific and medical advances, associated with Internet communications.

Interestingly, the evolving nature of our collective communications via the worldwide web has brought about an expansion in our ability to operate beyond, what some social scientists refer to as, "monochromatic" or single-purpose modes of living to "polychromatic" or multi-active pursuits. This is illustrated by our traditional Western attention to time-management, task-orientation and our automated style of leading and living.

In the larger society and our professional day-to-day modes of operation, we live by the clock. The concept of "time is money" plays out in almost every aspect of our daily living, both as a professional and as a consumer. Whether a schoolteacher segments classroom learning by ringing a bell or a project manager acts as the captain of time, money and deliverables, our culture has largely been aligned to moving from point A to point B in a given time period. The amazing impact of the Internet in its wide range of applications has elongated and coalesced "polychromatic" communications across time zones, cultures and most dramatically, in creating a forum for sharing ideas, concepts and diverse cultural practices. The stunning shift takes us from our limited time construct to communications across the planet, 24-hours a day, seven days a week.

As we move forward in the digital age of virtual technology, with its extraordinary advances in science, medicine and mainstream commerce, the importance of attuning to the human connection remains intrinsically important, especially in the enterprise of conscious leadership.

Without it we lose our ability to share in our pleasures, be encouraged, inspired and galvanize the people we lead and serve into successful outcomes.

BRIDGING COMMUNICATION and LEADERSHIP

EXPERTISE, PROCESS and UNDERSTANDING

In order to develop your own conscious leadership, you will need to find the intricate balance required to effectively communicate. But as we have learned in our own experience, communication is less a straight line than a three-dimensional hologram switchboard. This tripod-balancing act involves your ability to bridge the chasm between imparting your expertise with processes necessary to carry out a desired end result and a compassionate understanding of the person(s) with whom you are communicating.

This balance demands careful application, especially when you combine it with face-to-face human interaction. The power associated with effective communications always lies in the recipient's emotional resonance with the leader's message or vision.

THE LIMITS OF WEB COMMUNICATIONS

Web communications and learning tools, including webinars, blogs, and online classrooms, offer you a wonderful selection of options for your mission of communicating effectively. While the Internet has radically impacted our ability to communicate, learn, and process information, there are limitations to our ability to personalize communications via technology.

Using web communications as a primary driver of imparting leadership provides only partial connection with your employees. The most significant and transformative aspects of conscious leadership call for human connection, whether it is being present, taking risks or leading with love.

As a communicator, what is most important is the degree to which your words align with your actions. If you exclusively communicate via email, you are missing all of the subtle emotional attachment that your verbal communication offers. How many times do you need to witness email communications that fail to accurately demonstrate both the content of the message and the tone of your words? To misinterpret tone is to misinterpret meaning. This is a potentially destructive element that can seriously impede your ability to lead effectively. It then becomes practically impossible to stir the hearts of your employees, connect with emotional resonance or inspire loyalty.

Be consciously selective in what communications are delivered via email as opposed to face-to-face. Those items requiring simple answers such as "yes or no," can be easily communicated via email. For important informational messages that require either detailed responses and/or requests for high priority time sensitive information, you may choose to speak directly to your associate via phone and/or meeting. Where there is any possibility of miscommunication and/or misunderstanding of the content or tone of the communication, err on the side of contacting directly as opposed to quick emails. Confidential and highly sensitive communications should be optimized by face-to-face, if possible.

THE POWER OF NON-VERBAL COMMUNICATIONS

But effective communication is not just about verbal interaction. The strongest impact of human interaction is often what happens between you and another on a nonverbal level. Eye contact, energetic interest, body posture, direct attention, and nonverbal audible cues of acknowledgment all serve as communication. Interestingly, in the vernacular of the corporate world, nonverbal audible cues encompass anything from polite grunts (uh huh) to short phrase acknowledgments of "yes," "I see," or "got it."

As a leader, you might be quick to point out the importance of connecting with your customers. But many leaders are slow to demonstrate this same level of interest with their own colleagues. Is it possible that the pace of our business environment has devolved to minimize our own ability to stop the incessant internal taskmaster from slowing down enough to care? The challenge, always, is to take the time to get out of our heads and into our hearts.

My years of executive coaching have taught me that, at times, the most effective communications are no words at all, but rather an open heart and the quiet observance of those being coached. Structurally, as leaders within a corporate construct, we have playbooks designed to categorically identify steps for managing our business. Included in the playbook are well-defined orderly processes to employ when coaching associates, interacting with customers, and adhering to various human resources activities.

Follow the step-by-step guides and you will be successful, right?

Wrong.

It is not enough to just follow the playbook when leading others. In fact, one might argue that we could program a robotic manager to operate from an organizational playbook. Employees may get the message, but it will not motivate them one iota.

THE HUMAN TOUCH

The integral missing part of the solution lies in balancing your leadership communications to optimize the ways in which your associates receive your message. Your employees are human beings who desire the human touch. Not the hearty pat on the back or even the friendly handshake. What your associates really want--and will most respond to--is a touch of humanity that occurs in a shared look of understanding or a grateful smile.

MOTIVATION COMES FROM WITHIN

The best you can achieve as a leader is to create an environment where your associates feel motivated. Yet motivation comes from within each of us, not from an external attribute that we can control in others. As an effective leader, you understand and respond in ways that encourage a motivated and loyal work force. Your employees want to feel connected to the work they perform and to you. Every associate is uniquely different in terms of what motivates him or her. The trick for conscious leaders is to know what motivates each associate to create an environment that allows for his/her fully engaged participation. Success is then shared with the entire team.

LEADERSHIP STYLES

One of the most important first steps in leading a new group is to provide them with the knowledge of how to manage *you*. Think about it: Is it not unfair to let your employees guess the important aspects of your leadership style?

Just as you need to understand what motivates your workforce, your associates also want to understand how best to interact with you as their leader. Failing to provide your associates with a glimpse of what and how to communicate successfully with you diminishes clear and honest collaboration. The end result is never truly getting to the heart of human connection. The investment of time and leadership energy is a critical priority and your associates will appreciate your willingness to be real with them. It is always about the *relationship*!

Equally important is to discover how best to communicate with those being led. Over the years I have participated in a variety of personality, communications and leadership style tests aimed at identifying my primary style along with accompanying secondary and tertiary styles. Whether using the Myers-Briggs format,

the Blake-Mouton Managerial Grid, the Hersey-
Blanchard Situational Leadership theory or any other
system to assess optimal leadership styles, the true test is
in our ability to connect in meaningful ways to those
individuals we lead.

ONE SIZE DOES NOT FIT ALL

It becomes crucial to accurately assess your employee's
most beneficial method of connecting. Conscious leaders
show interest in knowing what is important to their
associates. Some individuals prefer a phone call while
others prefer a hands-off email or to be invited to meet
with you in your office. We commonly refer to some
associates as "high maintenance," but as I have learned,
some high-maintenance employees become your best
performers and most enthusiastic apostles.

Another aspect of leadership communications lies in
realizing that for many people, what we hold as natural
can be absent from their limited life experience. For
example, younger associates may not yet have the
business acumen to easily navigate more complex
interpersonal issues that come with employee
engagement. Cultural, educational and even
geographical differences can impact how you lead and

coach your associates. I know leaders who were raised by artists and have a wonderful ability to be creative in their communications.

I was raised in a household led by a military officer in the 1960s. As a result, manners, respect, protocol, and duty were simply expected of my brother and me. These characteristics are indelible attributes carried with me today, and help me to connect well with colleagues and customers.

As each generation comes with unique and valuable skills, attitudes and attributes, recognizing and embracing the differences in order to tailor your leadership becomes essential.

PRESENTATION MATTERS

The impact of communication involves other facets beyond words, including appearance, professional presentation, and one's ability to be present with openness, flexibility, and the intention of seeking understanding. The term "Dress for Success" has remained with me for decades. For whether we acknowledge it or not, others are impacted by what we look like externally. The important deciding factor is to what degree our external appearance melds with our internal self. "Dressing for Success" implies an appearance of confidence, assuredness and professionalism. The three-dimensional world we inhabit operates within accepted practices and norms, including the dictates of companies that employ us.

But you can function within this construct and still hold true to yourself. What we wear as our professional garb is only our outer layer.

As a young man growing up at the tail end of the Vietnam War, I was a fiercely passionate activist. In high school my nickname was Renegade. I always had an opinion, was eager to dole out advice and was sure I could change the world. This bigger-than-life attitude eventually tempered to realize that true connection required less aggressive and more attentive listening and learning. This transformation in my own communication style opened the door to successful collaboration and bringing together diverse and expanded outcomes.

LEADING IN THE PRESENT

SMALL THINGS MATTER

Emotionally, physically, and spiritually, you are one person. You are not separate pieces of the whole, but rather a sum of your parts.

Living aligned to your unique energetic self requires bringing all of you to your leadership, not simply those attributes your company demands.

In order to be a transformative communicator, you must be 100% authentic. You do not want to pretend to be someone you are not, or to believe something you do not support, simply because you want to make a good impression. Others feel your falseness. Set aside that which you fear and step into your genuine passionate self. What you say is not as important as how you live out your thoughts, intentions, and choices in your behaviors. When you do so while living in the present tense, with an open heart, transformation occurs.

Try taking small, but significant amounts of time to genuinely be interested in another human being. The small things make a big difference. Smiling, a warm greeting, thanking an associate for superlative performance, encouraging someone to try again, and actually meaning it when you ask, "how's it going?" all differentiate an outstanding leader from a run-of-the-mill manager.

NEVER ENOUGH TIME

Leaders who fail to find the time to be present with those they serve suffer a great loss. Our automated, fast-paced business world has created a sense of scarcity of time and resources. It seems that there is never enough time to accomplish all your tasks. We are constantly in lockstep with a buzzing BlackBerry, countless meetings, conference calls, and other duties that pull us away from the human connection.

But when you choose to live consciously, you will find that the time spent actually engaging someone else can create the opportunity for bonding, loyalty, and friendship. More than that: it creates the opportunity for sharing ideas, inspiration and encouragement.

Being a transformative communicator requires that you set aside your fears and instead step into your genuine, passionate self. Be present, be open, have a clear intention of what you are saying. When you communicate with an open heart, transformation occurs.

It never takes more time than you have to give someone a warm smile. Dare to be your brilliant and luminous self.

Conscious Leadership Principle #6:
BE A LOVE LEADER

*Follow the path that leads to understanding.
Only then, will you illuminate the way for others.
Once you open your mind and gain knowledge,
truth, you'll leave the darkness and enter into the
light of wisdom.*
~ Amaka Imani Nkosazana

In transformative leadership, nothing is more vital than the ability to lead with love. Over my years working as an executive in the banking industry, I have frequently chosen to bring this unusual concept forward with my peers and in my development of future leaders. To best understand the power associated with this conscious principle, you need look no further than yourself and your own deepest needs.

DESIRE FOR LOVE

What one human attribute do we seek most in our lives, from birth to death? Most would agree that it is the desire to find love, to share love and to enjoy the warmth of another's love. Yet for so many walking on the planet, the satisfaction of this desire is out of reach because we feel unworthy of love, fearful of its hold, or estranged by a Puritan heritage (at least in Western cultures) that falsely unites sin with love. Unfortunately, many settle for relationships that do not reflect their true passions or most desired expressions of love.

The net effect of living without genuine love is a life of darkness--an environment where nothing nourishing can grow. By contrast, those who embrace love, compassion, and understanding find their lives blooming with fulfillment and abundance.

When you think about it, it is nonsensical to imagine that leading with something *other* than love could be an effective way to run a business in which employees deal directly with customers. Yet we talk around the subject, carefully ensuring that we do not leap into the netherworld of leading from the heart.

PURITY OF INTENT

In large financial organizations, *purity of intent* is the latest catch phrase. But the expression begs the question, "What is purity?" Perhaps more importantly, "What is the intention?" We chase the almighty dollar as viewed by shareholder value, revenue, customer satisfaction scores, and quarterly earning reports. All of these preclude any real inclusion of "purity," which means a genuine expression of self, or "intention," which translates into our purpose as it is manifested by our choices.

We devote lots of time and dialogue in the corporate arena to the topic of leadership doing "what's right for the customer." In my experience, however, little room is given to actually providing this level of service to the customer. It is measured ever so carefully against accepted financial practices typically aimed at minimizing customer benefit, even when in response to a company error.

Before we can successfully have an organization dedicated to providing this level of accountability to our customers, we must first attend with genuine care to those we serve.

CARING FOR THOSE YOU LEAD

Do your associates know you care about them? If so, by what measures do they know?

WILLING PARTICIPANTS

Probably the best way to ascertain whether your employees know you care for them is by their willingness to participate in areas of the business you lead. You could also ask them directly how they feel about your leadership. I have worked with and/or observed many leaders who would be surprised to learn how disconnected their associates feel.

FAIRNESS, CONSISTENCY and ACCOUNTABILTY

When coaching and training future leaders, I emphasize the critical importance of leading with a sense of fairness, consistency, and investment of energy for all. A pitfall for new leaders is a primary desire to be liked by those they lead. In an attempt to connect in this way, they choose to be less direct regarding accountability, expectations, and performance standards. Notoriously, this new leader falls prey to creating unbalanced professional relationships with those who eagerly seek the attention. They often perform too much of the work themselves and establish what are perceived as unfair, inconsistent, and negative group dynamics.

Leading from the heart does not mitigate strong accountability nor does it minimize the numerous practical matters that must be attended to in order to successfully running a business. It does, however, alter the interpersonal relationships of those you lead and serve, both associates and customers. It ensures a genuineness and purposefulness in the leader's communications with his/her associates.

LEADING FROM THE HEART

Your direct report colleagues know when you are being real. They feel your genuineness and sense your capacity to care for them by your taking a moment to ask about their well-being, their family, their interests, and other matters that are important to them. Your nonverbal engagement is not hurried, but rather fully present. Where personal issues arise, you, the leader, do not withdraw, but rather engage with coworkers to better understand their situation with compassion. You listen deeply and reflect back an acknowledgement of meeting employees where they are. These small, but hugely significant attributes, separate transformative leaders from mere managers.

MEETING THEM WHERE THEY ARE

HOW *NOT* TO LEAD

I recall a time when my own manager was anything but understanding when it came to an employee's personal issues. One of my peers was suddenly called by his wife to inform him that their daughter had become ill and required a trip to the emergency room. She asked my colleague to meet her at the ER immediately.

The 40-year-old manager had no children, and was committed to operating an aggressive, results-driven sales organization. Responding to my peer's dilemma, the manager flatly refused his request to leave the office, saying: "You'll have to choose between work and family." The anxiety and stress brought upon him was unbearable to imagine, given that he had just learned that his daughter was ill. This response created a lose-lose situation: either the manager was going to have to work with someone who was far too distracted to be able to focus on work and produce good results, or risk losing a valuable employee. I have coached associates and clients that it is equally important to know how *not* to lead others as it is to know how to lead effectively. The example above clearly illustrates one method to avoid.

SUPPORTING YOUR ASSOCIATES

As a result of observing this and other negative leadership styles, I learned to honor and respect the associates I lead and serve by recognizing the importance of supporting them in a holistic manner, including their roles as parents. When a direct report employee comes to me alarmed by a call that his or her child is sick, my immediate response is to inquire how I can assist the associate in caring for their child. If this means finding another person to cover or shifting other resources, so be it.

The same holds true for those whose parents are struggling with the ravages of old age and require additional attention. As the primary caregiver to my dementia-stricken mother in the early 1990s, I know all too well how challenging it is to care for an aging parent. The emotional and spiritual duress can be overwhelming. Remembering my heart-wrenching experiences with my mother, I make every attempt to look for ways to provide support to those in similar situations. I can't emphasize this point enough: Compassion, empathy and caring are absolutely essential in supporting those you lead.

A measure of love and compassion does not break the bank in corporate dealings. Instead, it instills an *energetic vibration* that lifts people up rather than tearing them down. Tying this to the broader economic health of the company, healthy and cared for employees are significantly more inclined to offer their customers a differentiated level of service and care. Time and again, I have directly experienced the power of meeting those I serve with a genuinely loving and caring intention.

PERFECTION- NOT THE END GAME

It is important, though, to realize that at times this level of leadership engagement can fall short of the mark. Being fully present allows you to weigh options in order to transform an employee situation. But you may miss the target at times. You can lead a horse to water, but making it drink is another story all together. Some associates may not be willing to embrace conscious leadership at this time. They may have their own internal fires still burning that prevent them from opening up to leadership offered with loving care and a desire to enhance the professional relationship. But that does not mean that at some point the seeds you planted will not grow. I have learned to not let discouragement or failed attempts alter my intentions. Accepting my own imperfect humanness is critical, for in this acknowledgment comes the opportunity for improvement.

The effects of this style of leadership are to rally positive synergies in realizing that we do better when we pool our collective energies, rather than trying to operate in a go-it-alone, self-absorbed way. Leading with love provides a catalyst for inviting your associates to freely contribute their ideas, solutions and perspectives. When this occurs, an expansion of thinking and participation emerges, adding depth and shared ownership in the business strategy and outcomes.

THE POWER OF LOVE

You need to look no further than your own life to see the power of love when exercised from a genuinely open heart. Think back on your own "Kodak moments" in which you felt loved or expressed deeply felt compassion for others. These compelling moments remain a part of our memory. At times, each of us longs for the uniquely warm and wonderful feelings associated with unconditional love.

FALSE ASSUMPTIONS

Even though we all need love and support, curiously, in our professional lives, we think we need to be as independent as possible. Somewhere along the journey we learned that in order to be successful in the corporate world, we must be ruthlessly assertive -- dare I say, aggressive -- in order to achieve high performance, recognition, and upward promotion. We became accustomed to a survival-of-the-fittest mindset, where only the strong succeed in a harshly competitive world.

Amid the intensity of the demands placed on us within the corporate milieu, we have nearly lost sight of the fact that we human beings are, by nature, connected with each other. In this truth lies an amazing opportunity for meaningful human encounters and outcomes. Yet for a majority of companies, these opportunities are currently unrealized--or at best, severely limited by our collective myopia.

MYTH BUSTERS

Myths require busting in order to shift from unconscious to conscious. You can then infuse the higher vibration of love and compassion into your roles as leader.

Myth #1: *It takes too much time!*

No, actually there is always enough time to choose to care for another. The additional minutes required to genuinely inquire how someone is doing, how their daughter is feeling, or how they are progressing on a project, come back to you tenfold in bridging the chasm between worker and boss.-Despite our natural urge to live in the future or in the past, all you really have is the present moment. Whether you opt to spend the modest amount of time necessary to show your support and interest is entirely your choice to make.

MYTH #2: *Getting too close to my direct reports is problematic!*

No it isn't--not if you are consistent, fair, and equal in your access and care to all employees. Speaking from the heart allows you to be authentic and human with those with whom you work. This quality breaks down barriers to honest human connection by inviting others to do the same without fear of retaliation, chiding, or diminishment. I have often stated to those I lead and serve that my role is multifaceted. I play everything from boss to coach to brother to father to rabbi, priest, psychologist and even friend. Meeting others where they are is an essential component of effective leadership. It demands that you know the other person beyond what their sales numbers show, their performance appraisals demonstrate, or what some may extol as their virtues or challenges.

Ask yourself these questions:
- ✓ What do your associates value in their lives? Do you know about their family composition?
- ✓ When not working, what hobbies or special interests do your associates enjoy?
- ✓ How are they motivated? What are their passions?

✓ What aspirations do your associates have for their futures?

All these questions demand a level of consciousness and intentional connection to those you serve. If you don't already know the answers to these questions, make it a point to find out.

MYTH #3: *If I show that I care about my associates, I will be seen as weak!*

Not true. To *not* care about those you serve and lead is cowardly. Leaders who break the corporate mold to demonstrate honest love and compassion toward employees exhibit enormous courage and strength of character. By attuning to a higher vibration, creating an environment of genuineness, and putting into motion the energetic flow of caring, the workplace transforms into a rich group of human beings moving toward a bigger aspiration. The associates feel this shift, which in turn is transmitted to the customers they serve.

MYTH #4: *My customers come first!*

Not quite.

Organizations that seek to put the customers first are not wrong in their goal, but lopsided in missing the essential first step. Happy employees, who feel cared for, represented fairly by their leadership, and given top-notch support, are most inclined to carry that spirit of connection to their customers. World-class organizations recognize this essential dynamic in treating their internal customers--employees--with love and care.

Companies such as Aetna, Ritz Carlton, Microsoft, Costco, Whole Foods and Southwest Airlines all place a high priority on the well being of employees. For instance, Ritz Carlton's mantra is, "Ladies and gentlemen serving ladies and gentlemen." Costco, an industry-leading retailer, realizes the importance of their associates having holidays with their families and loved ones. Unlike their competitors, Costco closes during most traditional holidays. Aetna's, Mark Bertolini, has instituted yoga and meditational practices for his employees.

These are the frontline associates who directly represent the companies to their customers. A multitude of corporations and companies in our world fail miserably in creating environments where their employees feel well cared for, supported, and understood. Ultimately, the corporate culture provides the system in which leaders lead; however, we as leaders can make individual choices from within the structure of the company where we work.

LEADING FROM THE INSIDE OUT

In my own experience, I have come to understand the significance of choosing to infuse love and compassion into my leadership style and practice. I have chosen to express my strong feelings in this regard in executive meetings. While I took my peers by surprise at first, those individuals with whom I share leadership responsibility did not close themselves off to the concepts I presented. Rather, they have become interested in the relevant outcomes.

LOVE LEADER OUTCOMES

Caring is good for business. After I began employing the principles espoused in this book, the overall sales performance within my line of business significantly improved, customer satisfaction trended positively and associate engagement dramatically rose. Additionally, a number of successfully effective leaders emerged.

Leading nearly two hundred employees in the financial services industry has provided a rich laboratory in which to experiment. The weakness attributed to leading with the so-called "squishy" attributes of love, compassion, and understanding melts away in the face of significant positive outcomes.

FEAR vs. LOVE

We all live our lives on a continuum between fear and love. It is said that one cannot have love where there is fear. In this simple truth resides an important lesson for us as conscious leaders. In the past year, my coaching with managers has evolved to help them discover what holds them back from realizing greater success. Different people define success differently. Some are looking for monetary fulfillment for them and their families. Others want to be recognized among their peers. Still others want to achieve promotions or enjoy the security of working on a team with a defined goal.

THE DINOSAUR IN THE LIVING ROOM

Opening a dialogue with those I lead uncovers the fears they defend against in their everyday lives. I do not pretend to be a psychologist, but I do show that I am a loving and compassionate coach. I am interested enough to support the associates in unraveling the fears that prevent them from realizing their dreams. We all have fears. For many of us, particularly men, exposing fears feels unsafe because it leaves us vulnerable and open. The wounds that have created the fears--while in some cases minor--are nonetheless scary to expose, especially in a professional work environment.

MY WAY OR THE HIGHWAY

Take David, a very successful leader who had enjoyed great success year after year. As a young man of twenty-eight, David had built his success on an aggressive, directive style, setting stretch goals for his team and accepting nothing less than differentiated results. When I arrived to assume the role of market leader, David became my right-hand assistant, providing support and counsel in managing the business. After working closely with him and coming to build strong relationships with the many associates and teams, I became aware of a hidden truth: David had not only aggressively managed his team, but had customarily done so by peremptorily issuing orders, creating harsh and toxic relationships with many associates. He was seen by many as a self-aggrandizing, "my way or the highway" manager.

UNDERLYING FEAR

In subsequent coaching sessions with David, after exposing the "dinosaur in the living room" critical reputation he had created, I decided to try to guide him toward some self-discovery. I wanted to get to the root of David's misplaced leadership style.

"What are you fearful of, David?" My tone was caring and compassionate. Nonetheless, he looked back at me warily.

"What do you mean?" he shot back.

"Why do you feel the need to be so directive and aggressive with your associates?" I was truly curious.

Now David looked down, silently reflecting. I could almost see his spirit searching for something. Finally, he replied, "My father works two jobs. When we moved to the United States from Lebanon many years ago, my parents sacrificed so much for us. I need to prove my worth to them."

I nodded, affirming his experience. Then I asked, again: "What makes you think that you must be so hard and demanding on your associates?"

His eyes welled up. "I am afraid I can't live up to my father's standards," he said, his voice wavering slightly.

"Does your father demand this of you?" I asked.

"No," he replied.

"Does your father love you?"

"Yes."

"So why are you fearful?" I asked once again.

After taking a long breath, David looked directly at me. "My father is a very strong, firm and commanding man who works harder than anyone I know," he explained. "I want to be like him, but I'm afraid that I won't be able to live up to him. I admire and respect him."

Guiding David through this conversation led him to realize that the fear he carried with him was not as much about living up to his father's expectations, but rather attached to his own fear of being "less than," a feeling shared by so many of us living and working in this win-or-lose competitive world.

When he was able to separate his fears from the reality that his father loved him just as he was, David was able to expose the root of his misguided and inauthentic managerial style. The months that followed revealed that David had taken my coaching seriously. He learned to stop and listen to his associates rather than barking off orders as had been his style. Associates were asked for their input in decision making as well as in creative solutions to business challenges. His associates and the overall performance began to show measurable improvement. But most apparent was a visceral sense of positivism and cooperation that exuded from his associates.

FEAR OF AN UNCERTAIN FUTURE

Fear dismantles our ability to genuinely lead with love and compassion. Yet what a massive loss it is to live with one foot in trepidation and the other on safe ground. It prevents us from realizing a life of full expression and potential. Fear tends to be associated with future events that swirl from within the mind, fueled by the false ego, creating scenarios that in all likelihood will not occur or if they do, the outcomes are far different from the imagined disasters supported by our fear. When we are fearful, the ability to express ourselves in loving ways is greatly reduced. Fear also prevents us from living truthfully from who we really are.

As in the case with David, when I help my associates recognize that the boogieman is not under the bed, but rather located within a fear-based future, we open the door to the possibility of living in the present tense. When we stop the incessant chatter of a fear-based protective self, we give ourselves the opportunity to choose a different course of action: one that allows for the presence of love, compassion, and understanding.

Again, love and fear cannot live under the same roof. Choose to be a love leader.

Conscious Leadership Principle #7:
BE A SERVANT LEADER!

"Being others-focused instead of self-focused changes your worldview. Living in a selfless manner and seeking to help others enriches our very existence on a daily basis. Get your hands dirty once in a while by serving in a capacity that is lower than your position or station in life. This keeps you tethered to the real world and grounded to reality, which should make it harder to be prideful and forget where you came from."

~Miles Anthony Smith,

LEADERSHIP vs. MANAGEMENT

The traditional autocratic managerial style views leadership as management. Priorities are associated with completing tasks, checking off the list of deliverables, or delegating work to underlings to complete and report back. The framework of this antiquated management system considered the manager as boss and the workers as theirs to control, resembling a contemporary version of a feudal lord and his serfs.

Many years ago, while working within the telecommunications industry, I could already see the negative effects this approach created in the workplace. Employees, myself included, were taught that their main purpose was to make their direct report supervisor look good. This passé system of control fails to recognize the individual as anything more than a small cog in a corporate wheel, ultimately leaving the employee disengaged, disgruntled and diminished.

More often than not, these unhappy employees would resign from the company, thus negatively impacting the bottom line expense of recruiting, training and the cost of providing benefits.

Five Ways of Being

In *The Servant Leader,* noted business consultant James Autry outlines five ways of being that distinguish truly effective leaders from the rest:

✓ BE *Authentic*

✓ BE *Present*

✓ BE *Vulnerable*

✓ BE *Accepting*

✓ BE *Useful*

Paradoxically, while we customarily separate spirituality from the workplace, those leaders who dare to embrace the spirited essence of themselves and those they serve create dynamic and successful teams. In the context of the workplace, spirituality does NOT refer to or align to any particular religious belief and/or makes no qualitative assumptions regarding organized religion, dogma or standards. In this case, spirituality refers to one's unique spirit, as being an integrated human being, body, mind and spirit.

We see trending within large organizations to embrace a broader application of wellness for their employees. Aetna, one of America's 100 largest companies by revenue, under the leadership of CEO, Mark Bertolini, has introduced "mindful leadership" to his work force of 50,000, offering them yoga and meditation classes as part of a program to fully support employee health and wellbeing. More than one-quarter of the workforce has participated in at least one class, and those who have, report an average 28 percent reduction in their stress levels, a 20 percent improvement in sleep quality and a 19 percent reduction in pain. Mr. Bertolini's "mindful leadership" has also led to higher productivity of the workforce, gaining an average of 62 minutes per week of productivity each, estimated at $3,000 per employee per year.

An article published in the business section of *The New York Times* on February 27, 2015, observes that other large companies are offering similar wellness opportunities:

> "Aetna is at the vanguard of a movement that is quietly spreading through the business world. Companies like Google offer emotional intelligence courses for employees. General Mills has a meditation room in every building on its corporate campus. And even buttoned-up Wall Street firms like Goldman Sachs and BlackRock are teaching meditation on the job."

Important to Autry's thesis is that the various components of "being" are critical to transforming the workplace. While I may *lead* a couple of hundred associates in my current professional capacity, I never refer to these associates as *"mine."* I do, however, speak in terms of collaborating, working together, and serving those I lead. There is a non-negotiable understanding that my success is entirely predicated on how well the associates perform. Because of this fact, I treat them as my customers, providing them my time, energy, coaching, training, passion and understanding.

BE AUTHENTIC

As outlined in Conscious Leadership Principle #1, being real demands that we be our *authentic* selves -- not what our company tells us to be, but rather our genuine and spirited selves.

In my coaching, I often tell employees and clients, "You are never better than when you are yourself." When you are being the *true you*, the essential *"I am"* part of each of us emits the energy of connectivity and love that elevates those around us, as well as ourselves.

EXAMINE YOURSELF

Authenticity requires self-examination. As Autry states: "Being authentic is, first, knowing yourself, then being yourself. Authenticity derives from our deepest, truest selves." Opportunities present themselves throughout the course of your daily leadership. Whether in meetings or collaborating on various projects, before speaking or sharing it is imperative to ask yourself: "Do I care more about making a point to further the quality of the discussion/project or more about making an impression on those participating?" These two very different motives are worth exploring. The bottom line: How much do I care about being authentic?

When coaching associates, do you speak strictly from the playbook, never deviating from standard rote structure? Or rather, do you insert your own personality, style and thoughts as they relate individually to each associate, meeting them where they are and inviting them to share their own authentic selves?

Your employees know the difference. So do you!

My professional and personal life changed dramatically, as did my outcomes, when I shifted to simply being

"Michael." Now as a leader supporting and serving many associates, I consciously decide when interacting with an individual to seek authenticity. I do this by first exhibiting my own genuineness and then by asking relevant questions to help associates uncover their true selves.

AUTHENTIC ENGAGEMENT

By engaging in real human conversation prior to jumping head first into business topics, you are able to make a genuine connection that allows employees to feel comfortable and recognized. This simple, yet powerful, practice opens the door to creating a human flow, which ultimately encourages stronger allegiance and engaged associates. "How are you today?" as a starting point when accompanied by a genuine smile goes a long way to building rapport with your employees. Inquiring about an upcoming vacation, finding out how a child's sporting event turned out or commenting on some unique experience the employee has participated in, are quick and sincere statements that can bridge effective authenticity. Their defenses drop and an opening occurs through which light shines and your connection becomes a reality.

After all, as a leader you want to know what your associates think and how they feel about the work they are performing. Authenticity forms by infusing your own level of honesty and sincerity into the interaction.

BE PRESENT

Autry aptly outlines the second attribute of a servant leader as *being present*, discussed in Conscious Leadership Principle #3. Living one's life fully requires waking up from the passive autopilot unconsciousness of going through the motions. When we wake up, we become aware. When we become aware that we are aware, we are in fact conscious. And being conscious opens the door to unlimited possibilities, characterized by a whole set of choices not available when we are asleep at the wheel.

THE ADVANTAGES OF BEING PRESENT

When living in the present tense, we hear sounds, ideas, passionate stirrings, and others' views from a different level of perception and intuition. Hearing beyond the words to gain a better understanding of others provides immeasurable knowledge and opportunities.

I describe living in the moment as a blank canvas on which we choose to paint any way we want. Just as the Chinese word for "crisis" can be translated to mean "opportunity," your conflicts or challenges are opportunities with masks on them. The power of this leadership attribute lies in "choice."

THE POWER OF BREATH

As illustrated in Conscious Leadership Principle# 2, the unconscious act of breathing is a powerful tool for bringing you back to your center in any given situation. Physiologically, we shorten our breathing when stressed, keeping the breathing in our throats rather than in our center. Awareness of our breathing provides immediate relief, quieting the body and mind to provide a sense of calm centeredness.

So turn off the jumpy "energizer bunny" mind that dwells in the past and uncertain future. Breathe, slow down and be present!

BE VULNERABLE

Imagine for a moment walking into a boardroom for an executive meeting where the leaders sit down and open the dialogue by discussing the power of *being vulnerable* as a leadership attribute. This would be an anomaly of major proportions in most organizations.

Yet Autry points out that, "being honest with your feelings in the context of your work" is a guiding principle for the courage it takes to be vulnerable.

DROP YOUR DEFENSES

Certainly, dropping your defenses can feel like risky business. The payoff, however, is dramatic when done with genuine purity of intention. It is a picture-frame moment of letting your soul be visible to others.

One poignant example was the aftermath of a major event that occurred on January 8, 2011. That Saturday morning, the nation woke up to breaking news in Tucson, AZ, where early morning reports told of a shooter at the Safeway grocery store. A tragedy unfolded with six individuals murdered by a deranged gunman, with several, including congresswoman, Gabrielle Giffords, seriously wounded.

The Safeway grocery store at the corner of Ina and Oracle housed one of my banking centers. That morning, two of my bank employees had just opened the branch office and were ready to set up a marketing table outside the entrance to the store. Gabby and her team had also set up an outside table adjacent to the entrance. I received a distressed phone call from the Assistant Manager, Rick, telling me that there had been a shooting. I immediately proceeded to tell my wife about the incident and drove to the location to assess the situation and provide any necessary support. What I did not know was the extent of the shooting.

Arriving on the scene shortly after the brutal incident, I made my way past several emergency helicopters, through local police, FBI and the crime scene to support my two working colleagues.

Meeting with my managers on that following Monday, I let my professional guard down exposing my own vulnerability as I joined the managers weeping for those lost and wounded. Tears rolled down our faces as we joined together for a prayer and a moment of appreciation for the sanctity of life. The Tucson community was in utter shock. It was a cathartic and powerful exchange.

Not only have I found vulnerability to be an essential component of effective leadership, but an absolute necessity in developing intimacy in relationships. Your ego "straitjackets" you when listening to the incessant chatter telling you to be careful, to not say this, or to not do that.

This internal voice only stifles your ability to live with an authenticity that opens the door to living your life courageously.

BE ACCEPTING

The fourth attribute of a servant leader, according to Autry, is to *be accepting*. Bringing mindfulness into your workplace is foundational to the servant leader. As Autry points out, "...if you are to achieve the goal of servant leadership, then you must abandon any dualistic notion of winners and losers."

Acceptance of others does not require approval of any particular idea or proposal they may present. I choose to accept others for who they are in their unique selves. When facilitated with this underlying level of acceptance, disagreement becomes fertile ground for developing creative solutions, as well as building more secure relationships. Our increasingly polarized world is epitomized by political divides, prejudice and class disparity. All of these characteristics show how non-accepting we are as a human family. As a conscious servant leader, you can change that.

MORE ALIKE THAN DIFFERENT

Because, in truth, we are much more alike than dissimilar. We may not share the same political ideology, but most of us want peace and prosperity. We may follow different religions, but we can still enjoy each other's company.

There is no room in our human adventure for closed-mindedness, ignorance, prejudice, or any agenda that supports separation and distance from others who are different. Limiting beliefs about color, ethnicity, religious affiliation, sexual orientation, politics and many other topics separate us rather than unite us as a human family.

We all share the same emotions. Parents' love for their children is not limited to one nationality or part of the world. We all mourn the loss of a loved one and share in the joys of intimate connection. Love is not a geographical or cultural phenomenon. It is a universal reality.

ACCEPTING OTHERS

When we fail to open ourselves to others with different views and ideas, we let darkness rule our existence. This is not an external issue, but very personal and intimate for each of us. Over time, I have come to realize that in order for me to be successful, I need to accept others for who they are and look for commonality on issues. The starting point is always a friendly hello, and from there an open heart and mind.

Choosing to be accepting is a choice that is yours to make as a conscious leader. Divergent opinions and disagreement can be catalysts for important action. Try it out. See what happens.

BE USEFUL

The last attribute of the servant leader is to *be useful*. It seems intuitive that usefulness would be part of such a calling. However, I have witnessed many managers attempting to play leader while just doling out orders, as opposed to being player-coaches who are truly helpful to those they serve.

Being useful involves much more than directing the show. Are you advancing the efforts of those you lead? If so, do you add value to your team's performance?

We have the choice to build up or tear down those we serve. Employees need your vision, your passion, and your contributions to their success. Words matter, but not in a singular manner. When attached to actions, words come to life as fuel that powers associates' performance and inspires strong allegiance, loyalty, and purpose.

Conclusion

A human being is a part of the whole called by us universe, a part limited in time and space. He experiences himself, his thoughts and feeling as something separated from the rest, a kind of optical delusion of his consciousness. This delusion is a kind of prison for us, restricting us to our personal desires and to affection for a few persons nearest to us. Our task must be to free ourselves from this prison by widening our circle of compassion to embrace all living creatures and the whole of nature in its beauty.

~Albert Einstein

The world we inhabit is changing at such speed and frenetic acceleration that in order to keep pace we must ourselves evolve, not from the Darwinian thesis of survival-of-the-fittest and physical evolution but rather from the next step in the human story, conscious evolution. The choice of whether you operate from a limited myopic autopilot view or one of conscious awareness is yours to make. On one side, we propagate the current mainstream option of being victims of an unfair and harsh reality. On the other, an expanded, illuminated construct invites us, as leaders, to operate differently.

The 7 principles of conscious leadership are relevant not only in the corporate context but across a wide array of human applications from education to not-for-profit work, from community service organizations to worldwide peace-building enterprises. These human principles aptly apply to parents, spouses, friends and neighbors, calling us to a higher order: that of love, compassion and the quest for understanding. Where there is darkness and misunderstanding, let us be the light that illuminates our path.

Conscious leadership requires stepping into your true self, vulnerable, genuine and real. It demands courage and strength of integrity to take the risk of showing those you lead and serve that you actually care, that you are interested in their wellbeing, that you stand up for those you lead, and that you consciously choose love and compassion over a fearful, false self.

It is illusion to think and live as though we are separate and apart. The evidence of this folly can be witnessed in our everyday human interactions from our distain for the noisy neighbor down the street to the crippling dysfunction of our political system, from the fear-based corporate construct to the battlefields in the Middle East. Every time we separate ourselves from others based on either perceived or ill-perceived cause, we do damage to the human condition.

Tapping into the power of choice creates for us opportunities to evolve, not only for ourselves but also for those we touch. Our thoughts lead to our intentions that create our choices, which then paint the picture of our reality.

In Proof of Heaven, Eben Alexander, M.D., describes his own journey into the afterlife. His compelling and deeply relevant story guides us into the higher world of the divine. As a renowned academic neurosurgeon, Alexander confronts his own narrow scientific myopia when sharing his story, "What I discovered out beyond is the indescribable immensity and complexity of the universe, and that consciousness is the basis of all that exists."

Consciousness is not science fiction. Consciousness simply is. Living consciously brings us into the flow of connectedness, the rich shared milieu of soulful and spirited aliveness.

On the other hand, rote unconsciousness means acquiescing and accepting a reality that places you and me in opposition to each other in a win-lose framework. Rather than open up to wonderful opportunities and great possibilities, we then continue to propagate the status quo and cede our human potential in ways that are toxic, unfulfilled and well below the dreams and aspirations we once held as unfiltered children.

At the core of this thesis is love and compassion, two attributes that, despite their exclusion from the corporate playbooks, are powerful and energetic capacitors that can ignite amazing outcomes.

Throughout this book I have shared my personal and professional experiences with the reader as evidence of the differentiated approach offered by simply waking up, being present and living true to who you were meant to be. My own journey to this transformative realization came about as a result of years of meaningful collaboration with a skilled life coach along with my pursuit of a masters program in Transpersonal Leadership. This, combined with a passionate desire to make a difference in the lives of those I love and care for, including those I lead, impelled me to bring the authentic Michael into being. I am here for you.

You have the power! The ability to turn on the switch is within your capacity.

This requires courage and the presence of heart-centered honesty, and at times great vulnerability, to confidently quell internal fires, in order for you to be the real you, the higher you, the human being that lifts others up and provides a personal and professional roadmap to follow.

Dare to be more than the limits of your title and social status. In the present moment, you are the painter, the architect of your future. Stand up and be the most amazing human being you can be. Lead with love by your own example. Seek understanding of others. Invite them to share in your vision. You are called to be a conscious leader.

The time is now.

CPSIA information can be obtained
at www.ICGtesting.com
Printed in the USA
FSOW03n0736030815
9466FS